a golfer's dream

FOR THE LOVE OF THE GAME

If a man is going to have a mistress, let it be golf.

—*Helga O'Brien, Larry Berle's mother-in-law*

This book is about an extraordinary adventure taken by an ordinary man. It entails a 10-year journey whose only driving force was a simple love for the game of golf. Its inspiration lies in some of America's most beautiful landscapes. Its foundation is rooted in the generosity of all those fellow golfers who share in such a love. Its success was inevitable because of this ordinary man's willingness to do just one thing: ask.

I am forever grateful to have shared this adventure with my extraordinary husband, Larry Berle.

—*Annie*

FOLB · FRIENDS OF LARRY BERLE

Some golfers chase a single-digit handicap. You chased the Top 100. Others chase the seven summits...or is it really all about the chase?! I had even more fun celebrating each story of how you accessed your latest course than I did celebrating the completion of the goal.

—Todd Peterson

Larry, you already know that I will dust off the Bermudas at a moment's notice, wherever and whenever you are ready to produce your next quest. Thanks again for unlocking all of those Top 100 clubhouse doors and for allowing me to serve as one of your Top 100 wingmen for some really great walks and even greater memories.

—Dave Zubke

I hooked up Quaker Ridge for Larry, as I have a friend who is a member. Larry invited me to play Atlantic with him as I have a home in the area. Atlantic was notable because it was the final course on his quest. More memorable was Larry's interest in course history, design details, and the sense of each course being part of an overall golf pantheon. I never had a doubt that he would pull it off. It was a Holy Grail that would be reached for sure.

—Steve Ralbovsky

I have known Larry since 1970. While there has been much time and distance between us over 36 years, we have always found a way to have delightful times in company, be it on the course, having dinner, out for a show, or exploring Hoover Dam. His energy and humor are always at a peak, it seems. And the people who know him are better for it.

—Larry Hoof

PURCHASING INFORMATION

A Golfer's Dream is available for purchase online at www.golfersdreambook.com.

It also is available in many bookstores and golf shops.

greer

Designed by Greer & Associates

905 Park Ave.

Minneapolis, MN 55404

www.thinkgreer.com

Printed by Ambassador Press,

Minneapolis, MN

ISBN: 978-0-615-14575-4

ACKNOWLEGMENTS

I've always made a total effort, even when the odds seemed entirely against me. I never quit trying; I never felt that I didn't have a chance to win.

—Arnold Palmer

First of all, I want to thank Ron Soskin, who passed away in 2006 after a long illness. He was the very first person who stepped up and said, "I can help you get on some courses," and he did. Also, I want to thank my wife, Annie, who introduced me to the game of golf. She took me to Pebble Beach for my birthday, which inspired the entire journey (although that was probably not intentional), and supported me throughout my 10-year quest.

All of the people who helped me get on courses are too numerous to list here, although they are mentioned throughout the book. I also want to thank my friend John from New York who helped me immensely in getting on courses that I never dreamed I would be able to get on. He wishes to remain anonymous, but thanks, John.

Thanks to Susan Hamre, my editor. Her guidance was critical and she kept me going even during the weeks when I asked myself, "What are you doing, Larry? You're no writer. Forget this!"

Thanks to Ken Greer and Ed Engle. Ken is copublishing this book with me. Greer & Associates and Ambassador Press volunteered to print the first edition without any money up-front. "If it sells, then pay me." Please buy this book, so Ed gets his $$$.

Thank you all.

Larry Berle

FORWARD

Play the game of golf long enough and you will eventually dream of playing on the best courses in the land. Tiger Woods can do it by simply showing up at the first tee, but for us mere mortals, it requires a bit more time, effort and creativity.

One of us mere mortals, however, has accomplished it. Larry Berle, who has no affiliation to the game of golf other than a deep love for it, set out to play all of the best courses, and did so. More successful, even, than many of us golf writers who enjoy the occasional shot at a PGA Tour course, Berle not only cracked the list of Top 100 Golf Courses as ranked by *Golf Digest* magazine, he conquered it. From the most exclusive or expensive to the most extraordinary, he got on them all and played a round. If that is not every golfer's dream, it's close, and there are few who would turn down such an opportunity.

To test your game against the best courses in the country and hit a drive on the most beautiful and beguiling holes that the game's greatest architects have created is truly a dream come true—and Berle retells the tale of his decade-long quest. In addition to his experiences, the history and culture of the clubs and the people he met along the way, Berle chronicles just what it took to accomplish the feat. He received a round on Pebble Beach Golf Links from his wife as a birthday gift (which was the first course and impetus behind the quest), and he came by playing few others so easily.

Whether you are a kid imagining hitting it stiff on the final hole to win the U.S. Open at Bethpage Black or another in a long line of golfers who hopes to walk the verdant fairways of Augusta National before you are done playing the game, *A Golfer's Dream* offers insight into what that might be like. It's proof that you can only be called a dreamer if you don't ever actually live the dream.

—*Joseph Oberle, golf writer and editor*

For Ron Soskin and Annie Berle

a golfer's dream

HOW A REGULAR GUY CONQUERED THE GOLF DIGEST LIST
of AMERICA'S TOP 100 GOLF COURSES

by Larry Berle

dawn of a dream

Go confidently in the direction of your dreams. Live the life you imagined.

—*Henry David Thoreau*

"You are standing on the greatest finishing hole in golf!" my caddy casually informed me as I stood on the 18th tee box of Pebble Beach Golf Links. The 18th tee box is built on a small precipice that juts out over the Pacific Ocean with only a little split-rail fence between golfers and the water below. While I waited for the others in my group to tee off, I listened to the waves crashing onto the rocks, enjoying the Pacific breeze against my face and breathing in that distinctive ocean air. The 18th is a 548-yard par 5 dogleg left, hugging the ocean all the way up the left-hand side. I hit a sizzling drive up the right side, and as I walked up that famous fairway, I felt as though thousands of fans were cheering me on. I sensed that I was not alone but following in the spike marks of every golfing great who ever lived. I know it sounds a little crazy, but I felt among them. As I putted out, I wanted to tip my hat to the crowd and throw my golf ball to the five-year-old boy in the front row before I headed for the scorer's tent. Of course, there was no crowd, there were no autograph seekers, and there was no scorer's tent. It was just my foursome and our caddies and a few Japanese tourists taking photos of this picturesque hole. Emotion overwhelmed me, taking my breath away as the 18th green faded into the background. Johnny Miller wasn't going to stop me on the way to the clubhouse for the winner's interview, but I had walked in the footsteps of Ben Hogan, Arnold Palmer, Jack Nicklaus, and Tom Watson.

I have been golfing for 15 years. Once I dreamed of sailing around the world and diving into its exotic waters. I was in the entertainment business, and music and boats were my life. Then I met Annie O'Brien and my life changed forever. We began dating during the cold, snowy Minnesota winter of 1988. As winter turned to spring, our conversations turned to our plans for the summer. I talked about my love of sailing, from the rugged beauty of Lake Superior to the crystal blue-green waters of the Caribbean to my little scow on Lake Calhoun. Annie told me about her passion for golf. She had grown up in a golfing family and that's how she'd always spent her summers. "I guess we won't be seeing much of each other," she said. "While you're out sailing, I'll be on the golf course."

"Humph," I thought to myself. "What are my priorities: Sailing or this beautiful woman I'm getting to know?" It wasn't long before my dreams of sailing the major waterways of the world changed to avoiding the major water hazards of the world.

As Annie and I lingered over dinner one late winter night when the snow had finally melted from the fairways, she asked me if I wanted to play a round of golf with her. "Sure," I said, "why not?" I had played some golf in high school, maybe a dozen rounds, but certainly not any in the last 15 years. "My dad has an extra set of clubs he's willing to loan you," she coyly informed me. I borrowed his clubs and headed to the driving range a few times just to be sure I could make contact with a golf ball. The next weekend Annie and I played a par 3 course. I sculled a couple, shanked one or two. We laughed. Lo and behold, I hit a couple of good shots, too. She beat me soundly.

"Did you have fun?" she asked over a drink in the clubhouse.

"Yeah," I said. Already I was developing a case of golfer's amnesia, the good shots occupying a much greater space in my memory bank than the bad. "My dad said you can keep the clubs in the trunk of your car for a couple weeks if you want." Over the next few months, I learned just how well a set of golf clubs and the trunk of a car go together, but it never occurred to me that a trunk large enough to hold golf clubs would become a requirement in my future car purchases.

I became a student of the game and a regular at the driving range. I bought my own golf clubs. There was no doubt about it: I was getting hooked on golf. I learned that non-golfing friends do not understand a golfer's love for the game. Golf is like a political party; it seems to be the catalyst for relationships. I played around the public courses with my new friends. The camaraderie among golfing friends is a tie that binds, and the strength of that bond was a key to my success in getting on the private Top 100 courses that I eventually played.

It didn't take long to figure out that the road to improvement for a golfer is never-ending. I read golf books, took golf lessons, and endlessly discussed golf swings and golf shots with my golf friends. I worked at tee shots, iron shots, chip shots, and putting, but getting out of bunkers was one skill I couldn't master. One hot, sticky day at the driving range, my friend radio disc jockey Brad LeMay said, "Let's go hit some sand shots." I gulped and meekly followed him. Brad was determined to teach me how to get out of sand. We were in that practice bunker for what seemed like an eternity. When it was over, I could get out of the sand. I went home satisfied, exhausted, and looking like I had just crossed the Sahara Desert. Sand was clinging to the sweat on every pore of my body.

Eventually, Annie and I joined Hillcrest Country Club in St. Paul, Minnesota. Country clubs were desperately seeking members in the early '90s. There was no initiation fee; Annie and I were accepted as a couple, even though we were not yet married, and she was listed as the primary golfer (a few years younger than me, she qualified for lower dues). "Amazing," I thought. "We are moving up to the country-club set." I later learned that the club we joined didn't qualify us for the "country-club set" as I had envisioned it. Groucho Marx once said, "I would never join a club that would have me as a member." This club definitely would have accepted Groucho as a member. But our membership had its benefits: I played more often, took more lessons, and developed a new set of friends. I was out on the course all the time, and I grew to love the game. I got my money's worth out of that membership.

Annie and I were members at Hillcrest for several years. When Bearpath Country Club, a Jack Nicklaus design, was built in the Minneapolis suburb of Eden Prairie, we decided to join so we could play at one of the best courses in Minnesota. It was a very young membership, and we were all on equal footing trying to make new friends. We joined in 1995 when only 11 holes were complete, and it has been a thrill to be a member at Bearpath ever since.

Though I once dreamt of sky-blue waters, I now dreamt of long-drawing drives landing in the middle of lush green fairways and high-flying 7-irons landing softly on beautifully countered greens. Golf trips were on the horizon. We frequently drove to Brainerd, Minnesota, home to several beautiful, highly rated Robert Trent Jones, Jr., Arnold Palmer, and Joel Goldstrand designed golf courses.

My life took another fortuitous turn when Annie took me to California to play Pebble Beach for my birthday. What a magnificent trip this was! We stayed in Monterey at the Inn at Spanish Bay, where a Scottish bagpiper played outside the front door at sunset, and a glowing fireplace warmed our sumptuous room. It was truly a new world for me. We took the famous 17-mile drive and then drove down Highway 1 to Big Sur, a winding road with majestic mountains on one side and the Pacific Ocean crashing into craggy rocks 300 feet below on the other. At times you could hear the yelping of the sea lions on the rocky shore and feel the salt spray on your face. Wow! We played Spanish Bay, Spyglass Hill, and on our last day, the famous Pebble Beach Golf Links. Although I didn't know it then, all three courses were on Golf Digest's Top 100.

As we flew home, I mulled over the wonderful, almost surreal experience that Pebble Beach had been for me, especially the emotions I had experienced on the 18th hole. I looked out the window, daydreaming as Monterey slowly disappeared in the distance, and recalled that glorious feeling of walking up that famous fairway. "I want to relive that," I said to myself. The idea of playing the Top 100 was slowly taking root in my mind and my life. It was a way that I could experience that emotional high again and again. I announced to my loving wife that I was going to try to play the Top 100. She just shook her head in amazement. "Forget it, you goof ball," she said. "Let's just go home and remember how much we enjoyed this trip." Still, I dreamed that dream. Of course, I had no idea of the 10-year journey that would follow—and I certainly never dreamt it would lead to writing this book.

6

a golfer's dream

california dreamin'

PEBBLE BEACH

I'm a golfaholic and all the counseling in the world wouldn't help me.

—*Lee Trevino*

As I stood on the first tee of Pebble Beach Golf Links, I looked around at the many people taking pictures and milling about. I looked down the fairway, which seemed pretty nondescript from my vantage point. But what a day it turned out to be! Caddies in white jumpsuits handed us drivers (just like on TV) and we were off. The caddies carried our bags, a real luxury, and helped us read putts. I was surprised at how much help we needed. On the first green, I read a putt to go right, and the caddie assured me that it, in fact, went left. "Really?" I said. He looked at me like the grand master that he was and said, "If I had a dollar for every time a golfer has said, 'Really?' to me on these greens, I would have retired from caddying a long time ago."

Mountains and oceans affect the way a putt breaks, which can fool the eyes into reading something else. For the next few hours, I listened carefully to my caddie's green-reading advice and desperately tried to see what he saw. Sometimes I saw it, most of the time I didn't, but I learned a lot about what to look for in the greens.

The first few holes at Pebble Beach are typical inland parkland holes. The one difference, of course, is that they are the opening holes to the highly coveted Pebble Beach. Number 5 (which has since been replaced) is an uphill, blind-shot par 3. Some even call it the only dogleg par 3 in golf. Here, once again, I relied on my caddie and had a successful hole. As you leave the 5th green, you are on the threshold of the most dramatically beautiful and challenging holes in the world of golf.

Pebble Beach truly begins when you walk up the hill to the 6th green and stand on a bluff 75 feet above the Pacific Ocean crashing onto the shore. Number 6 is an uphill par 5 that plateaus on the ocean's edge, where a house used to sit to the right of the tee box.

Most people never saw the house because of the dense foliage surrounding it. Pebble Beach Golf Links tried to buy it for years from a woman who would not sell—especially to Pebble Beach. When she died, her estate sold the house to Charles Schwab, who resold the land to Pebble Beach Golf Links. He took the land where the old Number 5 had been and built a small palace. A new Number 5 was laid out along the ocean. The great golf architect Jack Nicklaus was brought in to design it. To see it now, you would think that it designed itself. It looks like it always has been there.

It is widely known that Jack Nicklaus has always considered Pebble Beach to be his favorite golf course. He's won five times here, including the 1961 U.S. Amateur and the 1972 U.S. Open. He even talks about how he has hit every club from 4-iron to pitching wedge on Number 7. The tiny 7th is one of the most photographed par 3's in existence and the shortest hole on any championship golf course. It is a 95-yard par 3, downhill to a green that sits on a spit of land jutting out into the Pacific Ocean. On a calm day, it's a wedge shot. On the windiest of days, it can be a 3- or 4-iron. On this calm day, it was a wedge and an easy par. There should be a sign on this tee box that reads, "Welcome to Pebble Beach," because this is the heart of the course.

Step over to the 8th tee for what some call the worst shot in golf: uphill toward an aiming rock and to a target fairway that cannot be seen (forecaddies earn their keep here as they stand at the top of the hill to see where your ball lands). When you arrive at the top of that hill, with a 100-foot cliff and miles of Pacific Ocean on your right, you face what may be the best second shot in the game, across a chasm with the Pacific Ocean roaring in and out of it to a beautiful green 75 feet below. On a windy day, it will test your nerves as you ponder the thought of hitting it out over the ocean, knowing (hoping) that the strong Pacific winds will blow your ball back over dry land. Annie had hit her tee shot into the right rough, and it was on very spongy ground. As I stood on one side of her and her caddie behind her, she took a mighty swing and the ball just mysteriously disappeared. We were all sure that it had not gone anywhere; the three of us looked all around and could not find it. The thought of it still baffles me. The 8th is followed by a couple more holes along the ocean, and then you turn inland for holes 11 through 16.

On 17, a 190-yard par 3 facing the ocean wind, I hit the ball into the rough just left of the green. As I approached the chip shot, my caddie pointed out that it was just about here in the 1982 U.S. Open that Tom Watson chipped in for birdie (his 71st hole), which propelled him to a one-shot victory over Jack Nicklaus. (They were tied and Nicklaus was in the clubhouse.) I have seen that shot replayed many times on TV. Watson is standing in rough over his ankles. As the ball rolls in, you see his surprise followed by his exuberant galloping around the green. That historic spot struck something in me: I was playing a golf course where the greatest golfers in the world have tested their skill, a golf course that every golfer in the world wants to play. I didn't chip in, but I did get it close.

Annie and I had played Spanish Bay and Spyglass Hill before Pebble Beach. I found out later that both courses were on the Top 100 at that time.

SPANISH BAY

Spanish Bay, designed by Robert Trent Jones, Jr., represents target golf at its finest. Nearly every tee shot requires a forced carry over the wetlands. Similar to Pebble Beach and located just down the road, it sits right on the Pacific Ocean, with many stunning ocean views. Because most of the tee boxes have very limited views of the fairways, you have to be accurate to play here and I found it frustrating. When I started studying the Top 100 list, I was surprised to find Spanish Bay on it. It wasn't long into my quest that it was dropped from the list.

SPYGLASS HILL

Spyglass Hill's first few holes are exciting and interesting as you play along the sand dunes of the Pacific Ocean. With barking seals in the background, the course seems quite lovely. However, after the fourth hole, it moves up into the woods, away from the ocean, and it becomes just plain difficult. The fairways and greens of the back nine are home to many deer. Some have so little fear of humans that you have to shoo them off the tee boxes. I was surprised to find this course on the Top 100, but Spyglass Hill has stayed on the list and remains in the Pebble Beach pro-am rotation.

raising arizona

DESERT MOUNTAIN RENEGADE

This is a game. That's all it is. It's not a war.

—Jack Nicklaus

One day I saw a real-estate ad in Golf Digest for Desert Mountain in Scottsdale, Arizona. Desert Mountain Renegade, one of the development's four courses, was on the Top 100. I called the sales office, knowing full well that the property was well beyond my financial means. I set up an appointment for a tour and then said emphatically that I wouldn't even consider buying a property unless I could play the golf course and fully experience it. How could anyone buy a golf vacation home on a course he's never played? The sales staff agreed, but I had to pay a guest fee. I made the appointment and hung up, thinking, "Boy, getting on the Top 100 is going to be easy." Troon Country Club, another Phoenix-area course on the Top 100, was not actively selling real estate, so I used a different strategy. Jay Norman, the head pro at my club, called Troon for me and got a positive response. I was elated, until I realized that getting on a course in the middle of the summer when it's more than 100 degrees in Arizona was not much of an accomplishment.

Desert Mountain is the only development that is home to six Jack Nicklaus designs. Renegade, the first course built there, is difficult. Its unique design includes two flagsticks on every green, and a couple of the holes have two separate greens. Renegade can be played as six different-length courses, depending on which combination of tees and flagsticks you choose. The longest is 7,515 yards, which at the time it was built in 1989 was considered extremely long. On the first tee, you choose either gold or white flags; the gold are by far the most difficult and many sit on small plateaus on the greens. The white flags sit on larger portions of the greens and are much less challenging and frustrating to play. We chose the white flags. After the round, we toured some real estate, visited some of the clubhouses (there are several at Desert Mountain), and saw some magnificent homes, all of which were way out of my price range. Needless to say we didn't buy any real estate, but it is interesting to note that Desert Mountain, now home to the six Nicklaus-designed courses, has become such a large development that some of its homes are more than a half-hour's drive from the front gate.

hello columbus

MUIRFIELD VILLAGE

They should have slippers at every hole at Muirfield and pass a rule that you have to take your shoes off before walking on the greens.

—Lee Trevino

When I think of Ohio, I think of Cleveland or Cincinnati, but Columbus is the capitol of Ohio and the state's second largest city. If you want to see the Santa Maria, you'll find it on the bank of the Columbus River in downtown Columbus. Where else could you find a replica of a boat that discovered America? And Columbus has another claim to fame. It's the only city that is home to four of the Top 100 golf courses in the United States: Muirfield Village, Scioto, Double Eagle, and the Golf Club. (Many golfers argue that the Scarlet course at Ohio State should also be included in the Top 100.) Since they're located in the same geographic area, you might guess that these courses would have similar characteristics, but in fact they're all very different.

In the summer of 1992, I took my first trip to Columbus to promote a k.d. lang concert. I had rented the Palace Theater, and the show was a virtual sellout. "Now is my chance to call these four clubs, trade them tickets for an opportunity to play their course, and I will be on all four in short order," I thought. As I looked in the mirror and rehearsed my pitch, I couldn't imagine anyone saying no to my offer. Fifteen minutes later, I had called four head pros and been turned down three times. The fourth call didn't accomplish much, however. After agreeing, the friendly pro said, "Are you sure you want Muirfield Country Club and not Muirfield Village

Golf Club?" "Oops!" I said as I quickly hung up the phone. The Muirfield Village pro also turned me down.

Not being a quitter, I decided to call the clubs' general managers. There was no general manager of the Golf Club, and the general managers of Scioto and Double Eagle were quick to turn me down. I was beginning to lose faith when I called John Hines, general manager of Muirfield Village and director of the Memorial Tournament. He was very friendly and said he would be glad to make that deal. "Yes! It worked," I screamed as I hung up the phone. I called the box office, had tickets delivered to him, and packed my golf clubs for the trip. John never used the tickets; in fact, I don't think he even knew who k.d. lang is, but he not only kept his word, I played Muirfield Village for free. Believe me nothing thrills a concert promoter more than comp tickets.

The k.d. lang show was a big success, so I showed up at Muirfield Village the next morning a little bit richer than the day before and thinking, "Life is good!" John gave me the VIP tour of the clubhouse and introduced me to Valerie and her daughter Vicki. He had asked them to host me since I was required to play with a member. There is an old joke in golf in which a player hits a bad shot and announces, "That was a son-in-law shot: not exactly what I expected." This mother-daughter combination wasn't exactly what I expected, but I was playing Muirfield Village, the No. 9 course in the country. So I headed to the driving range and putting green, and 30 minutes later I was on the first tee.

Valerie was in her late 30's, and Vicki was high-school age. They were from Chicago, but spent summers in Columbus at their Muirfield Village home. Dad flew in for the weekends. If golf is a metaphor for life, then these two were playing their roles perfectly. "Vicki, don't leave those putts short, putt it all the way to the hole!" Valerie commanded. "Mom, get off my case. That's the best that I can putt," Vicki would retort in disgust. Their sparring continued throughout the day. It was annoying at first, but as part of my quest was to be a good guest, I began to see the humor in it and soon could hardly keep from laughing. I'll never forget those two!

I hooked up with John Hines for lunch afterwards, and he explained that sometimes they need musical entertainment at the Memorial Tournament, "So I took you up on your offer because you never know when I might need you."

I have played many Jack Nicklaus designs, but Muirfield Village is by far his best. It is fantastically manicured, hardly a ball mark or a divot, or an unattended blade of grass. Number 18 is a beautiful 390-yard par 4 dogleg right with black-walnut trees lining the left side of the lush rolling fairway. I hit my tee shot into the right fairway bunker, directly below Jack Nicklaus' house. "I hope he's not watching me through his front window," I thought as I bladed my sand shot into the lip of the bunker and watched it dribble out onto the fairway. Then I hit a crisp 8-iron to that elevated green about 15 feet from the flag. "I hope you're looking out that front window now, Jack," I whispered as I proudly strolled up the fairway, imagining thousands of cheering fans surrounding this green on the final day of the Memorial Tournament. Were they cheering me on to make the putt? Or were they cheering Vicki for surviving a round of golf with her mother?

Three years later, when I returned to Columbus to play Scioto and the Golf Club, I had the privilege of playing Muirfield Village again. With my friend Bucky Zimmerman in tow, I was hosted this time by gregarious member Frank Beyers, Jr. Frank is a car dealer in Columbus. One call from my new friend John in New York and Frank agreed to host me at Muirfield Village. It was as beautiful and challenging as ever, and reminded me of why this course is in my personal Top 10. Frank had sprained his ankle, but Bucky and I played with Frank's son Blaine and his friend. Frank stayed with us the entire round, riding in his cart, talking on his cell phone, and using his 20-foot golf-ball retriever to hunt for balls in the water hazards. He must have found two or three dozen. At Number 12, a par 3 over a large pond and perhaps Muirfield's signature hole, Blaine said his house was on the 13th fairway. Frank called his daughter-in-law, and she brought out refreshments. Now that's hospitality.

As much as I love the place, there are plenty of golfers in Columbus who would never join Muirfield Village. Jack Nicklaus and John Hines run a pretty tight ship, and the Memorial Tournament is a high priority with them. The course is closed for a couple of weeks every year for the tournament, and intermittently throughout the season if Nicklaus feels it needs work. With the short golf season in Ohio, that is an understandable deterrent to membership.

rocky mountain high

CHERRY HILLS

It took me 17 years to get 3,000 hits in baseball. I did it in one day on the golf course.

—*Hank Aaron*

Playing golf in Colorado is a unique experience. The jagged Rocky Mountains completely define the terrain. It is a lucky golf-course architect who gets a call to design a course in the Rockies. All you have to do is route 18 holes through that magnificent terrain and make it playable.

I was first introduced to Colorado on the ski slopes. When I was in high school, I skied on most of the great hills of Minnesota and Wisconsin. But I got tired of the freezing cold, tired of the icy conditions, and disillusioned with what a makes a great mountain. Years later, my closest friend, Jack Bolger, twisted my arm to try skiing one more time. Jack and another friend Alan Shapiro were going to Vail. "Come on, we will take care of you," they said. So I headed off to Vail with them, where it was not cold, it was not icy, and I quickly learned what constitutes a great mountain. A love affair with the Rockies developed in my heart. That love brought me back to the Rockies many times, mostly for skiing, but eventually for golf. Getting to play the three greatest courses in Colorado was a real thrill.

Steve Thaxton, a close friend of mine, had moved from Minneapolis to Denver to become the assistant manager of KUSA-TV. The Senior Open was soon to be played at Cherry Hills, and the International was played every year at Castle Pines. Since these tournaments rely heavily on KUSA to promote events and help sell tickets, Steve had a good relationship with the organizers. That relationship got me onto these two great courses: I ended up playing with the organizer of each tournament, which led me to think my Top 100 quest would be no sweat.

On September 10, 1992, I met up with Steve's boss, Joe Franzgrote, the general manager of KUSA and a former GM of a TV station in Minneapolis. He brought along one of his top sales people. Even Denver golfers consider it a privilege to play Cherry Hills. We found our host, Steve Knowlton, the marketing director for the Senior Open, in the understated clubhouse. An avid skier, Steve was a paratrooper in WWII whose job was to set up reconnaissance camps in the Swiss Alps. After the war, he was involved in the founding of Vail. It was a fascinating story, as was his telling of Cherry Hills' history. William Flynn designed Cherry Hills in 1923. In its 70 years of existence, the course has hosted three U.S. Opens and two PGA Championships.

The 1960 U.S. Open at Cherry Hills is one of the most talked-about Opens ever. Twenty-nine-year-old Arnold Palmer was favored to win the Open, having just won his first Masters. On the opening hole, Palmer drove into a ditch and took a double bogey. At the end of third round, Palmer was seven shots back of leader Mike Souchak. On the final day, Palmer stepped up to the first tee, drove 346 yards onto the green 20 feet from the pin, and two-putted for birdie. He birdied six of the first seven holes that day for a 30 on the front nine and had a 35 on the back. Palmer shot 65, enough for a one-shot victory. And he had some formidable pursuers. With six holes to go, Jack Nicklaus was in the lead, but fell away. On 17, Ben Hogan and Palmer were tied, when Hogan hit a 100-yard wedge shot one yard short of the green into the water (after hitting 34 straight greens in regulation). Arnie's Army was born that day; superstardom was just around the corner, as was an explosive and unprecedented interest in professional golf.

Cherry Hills has a tame front nine followed by a challenging back nine. As the four of us stood on the 10th tee, I had to stop for a moment and take in the glorious view of the pristine fairway before us with the Rockies towering in the background under that incomparable Colorado blue sky. Steve told us about a round he played earlier in the year with a couple "good ol' boys" from Texas. As they stood on the same tee, one of them turned to Steve and said, "Sure would be a fine view from here, if it weren't for them fuckin' mountains."

Ben Hogan picked Number 14 as one of the finest par 4s in America, and Golfing Magazine called Cherry Hills' final four holes "four horrible hussies who revel in luring noble men to destruction." How challenging is 16? So challenging that in 1938 Ray Ainsley had the highest single-hole score on it in the history of the Open (it was the first U.S. Open held west of the Mississippi). He hit his 5-iron approach into the creek and spent an eternity getting it out. He finally 3-putted for a 19. I could have beaten him that day.

The course closes with two back-to-back par 5s, usually a big taboo in golf architecture. Number 17 is 565 yards to an island green set in a lake. The tee shot on 18 has a long carry over that same lake. Architectural taboo or not, the finish does not diminish the greatness of Cherry Hills.

By the way, Number 1 at Cherry Hills is also the first hole at Tour 18 golf course in Dallas, Texas, which is promoted as the 18 most renowned holes in golf "painstakingly reproduced."

CASTLE PINES

Golf is very much like a love affair. If you don't take it seriously, it's no fun. If you do, it breaks your heart.

—Louise Suggs

The next day, my birthday, I played Castle Pines, and what a grand present it was! There were just two of us: me and Jack Doak, marketing director for the International Tournament. Joe couldn't join us as he had at Cherry Hills; he has a TV station to run—too bad. Of course, if he didn't have that job, I probably couldn't have played Castle Pines at all.

Castle Pines has an unusual story behind it. Wealthy Colorado oil tycoon Jack Vickers had a vision to host a PGA tour event, and he set out to build a world-class golf club with that purpose in mind. Jack Vickers has two 14-club rules in his repertoire: the number of clubs in his bag and the number of clubs of which he is a member (pretty impressive). For 11 years, Vickers tried to purchase the land for Castle Pines, and he was finally successful in the late '70's. He then invited 12 of his oil-tycoon buddies to be charter members at $500,000 apiece (raking in a quick $6 million). These 12 took on the title of the 12 Disciples. Each of them was given the privilege of inviting a few of their friends to join, and voila! Castle Pines was financed.

In 1981, Jack Nicklaus was contracted to design the course (Nicklaus was then the world's best golfer and probably the world's leading golf architect), and the world-class Castle Pines came into existence. In 1986, the second part of Vickers' dream was fulfilled with the birth of the International PGA tournament, an invitational event scored on the Stableford system and offering substantially more prize money than any other event on the tour.

Castle Pines members are scattered around the U.S., and most have to travel to play here, so it's not usually a busy place. However, these members are privileged indeed, regularly getting to test their golf skills on a fine piece of mountain real estate perched 40 miles south of and 1,000 feet above downtown Denver. There are no tee times at Castle Pines. On this busier than usual day, a couple of foursomes waited on the first tee, all of whom seemed to be chomping on big stogies and talking in that Texas drawl about oil wells and oil futures. It seemed like a pretty good snapshot of the membership to me. At least I didn't hear any of them bad-mouthing the scenery.

Jack Doak and I headed for the back nine first. At Castle Pines, Jack Nicklaus built a challenging course with elevation changes, mountain ponds, and babbling brooks strategically placed to gobble up your ball. Golf balls fly about 10 percent farther in the thin

Colorado air. Number 10 is a 485-yard par 4 and almost as many yards down. Number 18 features another of Nicklaus' signature concepts: the double fairway, with a riskier route for longer hitters and a safer route for shorter hitters. I didn't do well on the back nine, but the front nine was another story.

Number 1 is a breathtaking downhill par 5 of 644 yards, then the longest hole on the PGA tour. You could stand on that tee box all day just to drink in the fantastic vista. I hit a long sweeping drive that had a hang time over these mountains that would have made even an NFL punter proud. My 3-wood was equally well struck, and there I was 130-yards from the green and still more down-hill to go. I hit a 9-iron to 20 feet and drained that 20-footer for birdie. "Yes! I birdied the longest hole on the PGA tour. Take that Jack Nicklaus." My partner joked, "Where were those shots on the other nine?" We finished the glorious round with lunch in the club-house, and I drove back to Denver to meet Annie for a romantic dinner to cap off a fantastic birthday.

a golfer's dream

a bite of the big apple

NATIONAL GOLF LINKS OF AMERICA

Golf courses are the best places to observe ministers, but none of them are above cheating a bit.

—*John D. Rockefeller*

"Hello, I'm a concert promoter. Can I play your golf course?" I thought it would be that easy. It never occurred to me that getting on the Top 100 golf courses would be such a challenge. I spent many evenings looking over the list, considering each course from different perspectives: What courses will be hard to get on? What courses are public or have public access? What courses can I ask my club pro to call for me? How are they grouped geographically, so I can make the most efficient use of time and travel? What courses are least likely to fall off of next year's list, in case it takes me more than two years to complete my goal? (It took 10 years!) Where will I be presenting concerts, so I can offer concert tickets to the head pro as a trade-off and play the golf course? At the time, I had concerts scheduled across the United States with artists including Yanni, B.B. King, Andy Williams, George Winston, and Sinbad. I was certain that good tickets to these shows would open some doors for me. I was mostly wrong.

My journey began to take off in 1993. The first thing on my agenda was a talk with Jay Norman, the head pro at Hillcrest, the club I belonged to then. He agreed to make some calls for me, but he wasn't encouraging. When I asked how it was handled when out-of-towners wanted to play Hillcrest, he quickly set me straight: It would be a rare occurrence, and our club would, in fact, welcome the income. For out-of-towners wanting to play Augusta or Shin-necock, he warned, it was quite a different situation. Those courses discourage, if not outright prohibit, nonmember play, but he said he could help get me on a few courses, such as Old Warson in St. Louis, where his brother was a golf pro.

I dug in and began calling some clubs to inquire about their policies. The typical response was: "You must be invited by and play with a member." When I asked if they could refer me to a member who might want to host someone on a journey like mine, their responses were polite, but I'm sure many were laughing at me with their pro-shop buddies after I hung up the phone. Some said they had been instructed by the membership not to ask any such favors of members. Very few said, "Have your pro call and we will arrange it," but when they did, I called Jay to work out the details.

Obviously, this was going to take some effort on my part. I wrote letters introducing myself and explaining my quest to boards of directors, general managers, and head pros. That, too, was a dead end. Every day I would devise a new strategy, and when it failed, I would start over. I just wasn't getting anywhere.

One day I had lunch with my friend Ron Soskin, a music attorney based in Minneapolis and an avid golfer and tennis player. Not only was he enthusiastic about helping me reach my goal, he had some close friends from his law-school days who were members at some of the courses I wanted to get on. He called Larry Hilbert, then the tennis pro at Piping Rock on Long Island. Later that week I got a call from Larry: "What can I do to help?" I gave him the list of courses in his vicinity and some dates that I could travel to New York. In a few days, he called me and said, "I have you set to play National Golf Links and a few others, too, including Winged Foot." I was overwhelmed. I accepted the concept of trial and error, but I now understood that I was going to have to apply big doses of persistence to trial and error to reach my goal. I developed a new philosophy: Trial and error eventually must lead to trial and success!

Fourteen of the Top 100 courses are located within 80 miles of

New York City. An amazing fact! The New York area has hosted 21 U.S. Opens, nine PGA Championships, and 19 U.S. Amateurs, just to name a few. To me, New York City means the Empire State Building or the Statue of Liberty, not golf courses. Never before had I entertained the thought of hauling my golf clubs to a midtown Manhattan hotel. Now, in pursuit of my quest, I have done it many times. Since all of the courses are in bedroom communities and suburbs around the city, I had hoped to line them up back to back and blast through them in a single two-week trip, or even faster if I could play two in a day. Nothing was further from reality. For example, there are two golf courses at Winged Foot, just 15 miles north of New York City, and both are in the Top 100. They share a fence line with Quaker Ridge. It took three separate trips to play them, and those trips were several years apart, but the people I met and the things I learned on each of those trips were well worth the delays. A couple of years later, I played Quaker Ridge and Stanwich in one day. Only 30 miles apart, the courses are in two different states, another cool fact.

A few days after Larry Hilbert's call, Annie and I were off to Long Island. South Hampton is a long drive from New York City, but the National Golf Links is a beautiful course when you finally get out there. And just how did we get there? A close friend of Larry's is a member of the National Golf Links of America, which is known on Long Island as "The National." His membership privileges allowed him to sponsor us "unaccompanied." That proved to be very true indeed. We didn't see another soul on the course.

We had stayed with Annie's sister in New Jersey, and gotten up at the crack of dawn for the four-hour drive to Southampton. As we turned down the driveway to National Golf Links, we also could see its more famous next-door neighbor, Shinnecock Hills. The National is a very simple place, golf and only golf. Founded in 1908, it was one of the first golf courses built in the United States. That it was designed by Scotsman C.B. Macdonald comes as no surprise. Annie said it looked very much like a Scottish course, only 40 degrees warmer. We went to the clubhouse, which had the feel of someone's home, where we signed in and were directed to the pro shop, barely big enough for the pro and a small selection of golf merchandise. The assistant pro, John, said the first tee was all ours whenever we were ready. He directed us to a driving range that would have been crowded with more than five or six people on it. We warmed up and returned to the first tee in our cart.

Annie and I both hit good opening drives, or so we thought. The first fairway is a blind shot, and as we left the tee, I asked John, "How are the yardages marked out on the course?" "They're not," he replied. "We play golf here the old-fashioned way: no yardage markings." I gulped. "Now what do I do?" I thought. "I've never encountered this before." "Do you have a yardage book?" I asked. "I may have a cheat book in the back," he replied scornfully. He soon returned with a book in which yardages were marked from various bushes, trees, and bunkers. I knew then that we should have taken a caddie, but we were already off in our cart.

Golfers who are familiar with the great courses of Long Island claim that the National is a much better golf course than Shinnecock Hills. Its' ranking suffers because it's not long enough for PGA tour play, and because Golf Digest panelists are not allowed to play without a member. Fewer panelists who vote means lower ratings. We found the National to be a fantastic course with a hole that plays over a road (patterned after the famous road hole of St. Andrews), and with bunkers so deep that you enter and exit them via a small stepladder. (Not that I got in one, but I did drop a ball in a couple of them to see how menacing they were, and they were plenty menacing.)

The National opens with a 300-yard par 4 and a blind tee shot. I smoothed a 3-iron to the middle of the fairway and followed it with a 9-iron to the green. Two putts later I had par on Number 1 at the National. The course features many holes with blind shots, double fairways, deep bunkers, and plenty of wickets just off the fairways. As we played, I studied our "cheat book," trying to determine yardages. I resolved to learn to read yardages by looking at them, a skill that I have since developed to some degree, but not enough to trust club selection. C.B. Macdonald re-created some of the famous holes of Great Britain at the National. The road hole from St. Andrews (Number 7) and the redan from North Berwick are his most well known designs. Many of America's early golf architects frequently visited the National to study its challenging and enduring features. The redan, for example, is probably one of the most copied holes in history. You may have played one without knowing it: a medium-length par 3, the green running diagonally from front right to back left, with a large, deep bunker fronting it. The contour of the green falls away in the rear, so the forward right pin position is very difficult to reach. Number 10 is called Shinnecock, as it shares a fence line with its famous neighbor. I strained to see as much as I could across that fence line, not knowing if I would play there tomorrow or some day in the future.

I ended the day with a 92 on the par 73 course and a new appreciation of the game. Estimating yardages brings another level of course perception into play. I learned that sky color, green contour, pin height, and hazards in the foreground can fool the eye, and that caused me to observe details on the course I otherwise would not have noticed. So I asked myself, "If people played golf for years without having yardage markers, could I learn to play golf that way, too?" I tried to walk up slowly to shots, look at them without yardage information, make my best guess, pull a club, and hit a shot. It was more trial and error, followed by some trial and success. My next step was to estimate yardage, then look at yardage markers to see how close I had come. Over the next few months, my skill improved. It's amazing how your power of observation on a golf course increases in this process. When I asked other people if they had ever tried it, only a few had. If you've never tried it, I recommend it. Don't get attached to your score. Just keep reminding yourself what your learning goals are for the day.

After we finished, I told the only other person in the locker room about my quest. "I'm a member at Maidstone, just down the road," he said. "Call me and I'll take you there." "Yes!" I thought to myself. He gave me his card: Senior VP Chase Manhattan Bank. I was impressed. I knew Annie wanted to take a shower, so I asked him where she could find the women's locker room. "I've been a member here for 10 years," he said, "and I don't even know if we have a women's locker room." Now that's women friendly! In the meantime, Annie had found a chair and shower in a far corner of the building. I did call him a few weeks later about Maidstone, called him two or three times in fact. He never returned my call.

Annie and I hopped in the car and started our three-hour drive to White Plains, near Winged Foot, where we found a hotel and got a good night's sleep.

WINGED FOOT EAST

Give us a man-sized course.

—*Winged Foot founders to course architect A.W.Tillinghast*

Annie and I woke early in the White Plains Hotel, just a few miles from Mamaroneck, New York, near Bedford, where my Great Aunt Josephine used to live. The phone rang: "Good morning, Bill O'Hara here. Are you ready for your round at Winged Foot?" "It's awfully nice of you to offer to take two strangers to play golf at your club," I said. "Twist my arm," Bill said. "It's a beautiful day. I can't think of a better way to spend it. By the way, wear long pants, one of those silly club rules. Meet me around 11:30. We'll have lunch and then play." I'd heard of club dress codes, but I'd never before been asked to wear long pants to play golf.

"And I hope you want to walk," Bill added. "Winged Foot does not allow golf carts, and we have a caddie program we are very proud of." I later heard the story of King Hassan II of Morocco who came to play Winged Foot with a significant entourage, and they all walked to the first tee with pull carts. The caddie master told the king pull carts weren't allowed and then assigned a caddie to each member of the group. I wonder if the king of Morocco had ever been spoken to like that before.

It was a two-mile drive from our hotel to Winged Foot, where there are two courses, both on the Top 100: one is ranked in the

20's, and the other is No. 6. We were excited. We took the back entrance, and the striking clubhouse I had seen on television during the U.S. Open appeared before us. We perused the golf shop and met Bill, who said, "It's such a beautiful day! Let's forget lunch and go play golf."

Bill was 49 years old and a 6-handicap, but at the turn he was even par, a stellar round for him. You could see the excitement all over his face. I was playing well also, until I hit the middle of the back nine and my game came unglued. Every fairway at Winged Foot is lined with trees, and if you're not in the fairway—in many cases, on the correct side of the fairway—you've got problems. On Number 12 or 13, Bill hit an incredible 1-iron shot 225 yards to within five feet of the par 3's hole. Bill's was the only ball in our party to hit the green, but when we got up there, we found two balls on the green. The other had just landed, drifting over from another fairway. The golfer who showed up to claim it was Donald Trump, hair disheveled and growing a gut. Bill knew him and introduced us to "The Donald," who said, "I'm playing with a guy from *Golf Magazine*. He's doing a story on me." Annie was excited to meet him.

Since Winged Foot has two courses on the Top 100, we were hoping Bill would invite us to play the other one. He did the next best thing. As he pointed out the par 3 10th on the West course, which many consider the finest par 3 in the United States, he said, "Come on, there's no one on the tee at Number 10 West. This is the best hole out here. Let's play it and then go in." The tee overlooks a sloping green with bunkers on the front corners. I soon found out they were devilish bunkers to escape.

We had a bite to eat. Bill works in international trade helping people buy and invest in Russian businesses. He introduced us to a fellow member who had played in a couple of U.S. Opens and a Masters. "We played each other in the club championship 20 years ago," Bill said. "I birdied the first five holes and he still beat me." We took a tour of the clubhouse and admired the memorabilia, including a scorecard signed by Babe Ruth, who played here and shot 82, and a photo of Fuzzy Zoeller waving a white towel in the 18th fairway. In the 1984 U.S. Open, Fuzzy and Greg Norman drew into a tie on the 71st hole. Norman, who was one group in front of Zoeller, hit his ball into the grandstand on 18, took a drop and sunk a 40-foot putt for par. Zoeller heard the roar of the crowd, thought Norman had putted for birdie, and waved a white surrender towel. Fuzzy went on to par the hole and force a playoff, which he won handily.

Along the way, I asked everyone we met if they knew any members at Quaker Ridge, the other Tillinghast course that shares a fence line with Winged Foot. No one volunteered so much as an acquaintance. I learned that Winged Foot has a mostly Roman Catholic membership, while Quaker Ridge has a primarily Jewish membership. Annie and I jumped in the car for the long drive back to her sister's house in New Jersey. As we left Winged Foot, I looked longingly at the West course, which I knew I would return to play one day.

do you know the way to monterey?

CYPRESS POINT

We had a membership drive at Cypress Point one year, we drove out 50 members.

—Bob Hope

If I had to choose to play on only one golf course for the rest my life, I would play Cypress Point. In November 1993, my new friend Larry Hilbert, who lives on Long Island in New York, arranged for me to play Cypress Point on the Monterey Peninsula in California. Larry's the guy who also arranged for me to play National Golf Links and Winged Foot. Now he had arranged for me to play on the opposite side of the country. His father-in-law is a member at Cypress Point and sponsored my round there. I've never met Larry in person, but I will be forever grateful to him for helping me achieve my goal.

I was a very popular person with my golf buddies at home in the weeks leading up to my Cypress Point tee time. Cypress Point allows two unaccompanied foursomes every morning between 7:30 and 8:30, so I could bring three friends of my choosing to play on one of the most beautiful courses in the world. I invited Jeff Brown, Gary Albrecht, and Rob Rohe. At the last minute Jeff Brown canceled. (I don't know what his conflict was, but it had to be substantial.)

After a round the previous day at Carmel Valley Ranch, we got up at the crack of dawn like three excited little kids, stopped at the Spyglass driving range to warm up, and arrived at the Cypress Point clubhouse, which Sandy Tatum, former president of the USGA, calls

"The Sistine Chapel of Golf." The clubhouse isn't much bigger than my house, and aside from the pro behind the counter, I don't think the pro shop could fit much more than a foursome on the floor. We went into the tiny locker room and checked the lockers for names we recognized. I found a couple of winners: Bob Hope and Clint Eastwood.

Cypress Point is a private club that gets almost no play. It sits just a few hundred yards down the ocean from its cousin Pebble Beach, which gets all the play that can be squeezed into daylight. When the Pebble Beach National Pro-Am was founded, it was called the Crosby Clambake (founded by Bing Crosby) and featured play at three courses—Cypress Point, Pebble Beach, and Monterey Peninsula Country Club (later replaced by Spyglass) —and lots of celebrity amateurs (mostly Bing's buddies). It was the first stop on the PGA tour to be played on multiple courses. When the PGA tour demanded that tour courses have "diverse" memberships, Cypress Point quietly excused itself to be replaced by Poppy Hills.

As we finished up on the practice green and stepped to the first tee, a small commotion erupted on the driveway beside us. A limo, a van, and two other vehicles arrived, and bodyguards quickly emerged from the vehicles to secure the area. When the area was secured, the ambassador to the United States from Singapore emerged from the limo. Ten minutes later they teed off, with the bodyguards always playing one hole ahead. A few minutes later, we followed.

On the first tee, just a stone's throw from the clubhouse, the caddie pointed me over the hedge to the first fairway. My first shot at one of the most coveted golf courses in the world was a blind shot over a hedge, as if I was hitting it into my neighbor's yard. The caddie explained that the hedge is there to protect the road below it. I hit my 2-iron, and the ball was barely launched when my caddie called out, "Reload." It had gone right into the driving range, which is out of bounds. My mulligan was right down the center. My second shot was right of the green in the ice plant. I hit a very good pitch shot, but not quite good enough. "One foot from glory," yelled my caddie, as my ball fell a foot short in the bunker fronting the green.

I had informed my caddie that one of my goals at Cypress was to practice reading yardages, but every time we approached my ball he would bark out the yardage —out of habit, I'm sure. Once he finally got with my program, I would try to estimate the distance to the flag from my ball, announce my guess to my caddie, and he would respond with the proper yardage. On some shots, I was way off, but as the day went on, I got better and a few times got lucky enough to get it right. Although my progress was slow, I realized this was skill I could master—if I worked at it.

Alister MacKenzie, one of golf's great architects, designed Cypress Point in 1928. Even though it breaks many of the basic tenets of golf-course design —the first hole plays across a road I'm sure didn't exist in 1928, and there are two back-to-back par 5's on the front nine and two back-to-back par 3's on the back nine —Cypress Point ranks consistently in the Top 5 of every golf publication's top courses list. Robert Louis Stevenson once said, "Monterey Peninsula is the most felicitous meeting of land and sea in creation." Its emerald-green fairways wind through the rugged hills and dunes of the Monterey Peninsula lined with beautiful pine and cypress trees. Many deer and elk call these fairways and greens home. There are three par 5's on the front nine and all are risky, though not long. Holes 8 and 9 are on everyone's list of great par 4's. Number 8 is a 345-yard, 90-degree dogleg right, cut through the rolling dunes to a plateau green. Number 9 is less than 300-yards, but 300 of the most challenging yards in golf, especially when the wind is blowing, as it usually is.

Then we headed into what may be the greatest back nine in golf. We walked off the 14th green and across the road toward the ocean and arrived at the tee box of Number 15, a 127-yard par 3. It's the cute little brother to Number 16's brutish big brother, another par 3 of 219 yards. Both are carries over a crevasse with the crashing surf of the Pacific Ocean below; however, one is a 9-iron (on a windless day) and the other is a driver. Sixteen is the most photographed hole in golf, and while it was on the PGA tour, it was consistently rated the most difficult hole on the tour. Even Gary McCord said it is the only hole on the PGA tour that caused him to lose sleep the night before he played it. The 17th, which some say is the best hole in the Monterey area, is protected by a stand of gnarly cypress trees in the landing area and skirts the craggy Pacific cliffs all the way to the green. Unfortunately, Number 18 is as weak as 17 is strong, but you can't have everything. Gary birdied 15 and parred in. I bogeyed 15 through 17 and was damn happy to do so.

if you're going to san francisco

SAN FRANCISCO GOLF CLUB

They say that golf is like life, but don't believe them. Golf is more complicated than that.

—*Gardner Dickenson*

As I headed out the door, Mike Assum, a friend I was staying with in Carmel, said San Francisco Golf Club does not deserve its notoriety: "I'll be interested to see if your assessment of it is the same as mine."

I drove up to Palo Alto to meet Bill Beasley. Earlier that summer, when I was paired with Bill at a charity golf tournament in Minneapolis, he mentioned that he had a good friend at San Francisco Golf Club. He was the first person I'd met who knew someone there, so you can bet I followed up with him on the phone a couple of weeks later, and he arranged this golf date.

Dick Cannady was our host, a business associate of Bill's. I thanked him for inviting me, and we were off to the first tee, accompanied by Misha Yero. My goal on this course was to remember the many holes and shots as clearly as possible when the round was over. After each hole, as I was jotting down my score, I would review the previous hole in my mind and, when time permitted, recall the past few holes to refresh my memory. I closed my eyes and tried to visualize my last few moments on the course: What lines the fairway? Where are the bunkers? How wide is the landing area? What is the view from here? What trouble guards the green? What shots did I take? What was the green like? When I finished, I could remember almost every hole and almost every shot, a huge improvement over my normal round. My aim throughout my quest was to be an entertaining guest, so perhaps this was a self-indulgent exercise. I hope my concentration wasn't misconstrued as unfriendliness, and I don't think it was, but after this round, I refocused on my goal to be "America's Best Guest" once again. It was a goal that paid big dividends on my quest, because people who enjoyed playing with me were more likely to refer me to their friends at other golf courses I wanted to play.

Mike Assum believes San Francisco Golf Club—only 6,600 yards from the tips and par 71—is not in the same league as Olympic Club, which has hosted many major championships. However, given the choice, I would much rather play San Francisco Golf Club. It sits up higher in the city, with occasional views of both the Pacific and the Bay to the east, and its many elevation changes offer terrific city views. A.W. Tillinghast designed the course in 1918, and I have become a real fan of his work. San Francisco membership is very small, and they like to keep it that way. I was fortunate to have made a connection with Bill and Dick. If you ever have the opportunity to play there, do so.

OLYMPIC CLUB

Eighteen holes of match play will teach you more about your foe than 18 years of dealing with him across a desk.

—Grantland Rice

Olympic Golf Club is a much-storied course, just a few miles down the road from the San Francisco Golf Club. Olympic was founded in 1893 as an athletic club in the city of San Francisco. In 1924, the club acquired land bordered by the Pacific Ocean and Lake Merced to build 36 holes of the Lake and Ocean courses. The Lake has hosted three U. S. Opens, the most recent in 1987, and the Tour Championship in 1993. Because there are no water hazards and only one fairway bunker, some call the 6,808-yard par-71 Lake course one of the world's longest short courses.

My closest friend, Jack Bolger, a non-golfer from Minneapolis, was anxious to help me on my quest. "One of my clients, Mike Butler, president of the San Francisco Gift Mart, is a member at Olympic Club. Let me see what I can do," Jack said over dinner one night. When he asked if Mike would host me, Mike said, "I hardly ever play anymore, but have him call me. I'll be glad to play a round with him."

When I met Mike at the driving range, I learned that 30 years earlier he had played on the PGA tour. He wasn't particularly successful, but it is quite an accomplishment just to play at that level. Mike is more interested in horses now and only plays a couple of times a year, mostly what he describes as "business golf." I feel privileged that he was willing to spend a day playing golf with me.

On the first tee, I headed toward the member tees (6,500 yards). "That should be enough for me," I said. Mike looked at me with unflinching conviction and said, "You don't fly halfway across the country to one of the world's great golf courses and not play the whole thing." So I reluctantly went back to the tips. Just before we teed off, the pro came out from the shop to talk to Mike. "A guy in town on one of the PGA's development tours wants to play Olympic," he said. "Mike, since you played on the PGA tour at one time, would you mind if he joins you?" "No problem," said Mike. I was both intimidated and excited at the same time. We introduced ourselves and teed off immediately. These guys hit rockets, and I hit my usual 220-yard drive up the fairway. It turned out to be one of the most interesting rounds on my quest. As Mike began reminiscing about his bygone days on the PGA tour and they compared experiences then and now, their competitive juices started flowing and their game was on. Mike shot four over par and our new friend shot two over; I was a fly on the wall with a very high score. We all exchanged phone numbers, and our new friend said, "If you want to follow me in the paper, my results appear in USA Today every Wednesday." As I walked to my car, I was still shaking my head. "How does a guy shoot 75 when he plays only a couple times a year?"

A year later, I got a call from our third that day. "Hi, it's Jerry Kelly. I played golf with you at Olympic. I'm on the PGA tour now. You're in the concert biz right?" "Yeah" I said. "I want to take my wife to see Jimmy Buffet in Miami. Can you help me get tickets?" I did, and I've followed his career closely ever since. Last year, Jerry Kelly won more than $2 million on the PGA tour. I've seen Jerry a couple times since, at the Greater Milwaukee Open and the Masters.

l.a. confidential

RIVIERA COUNTRY CLUB

Tiger Woods is an inspiration to anyone who loves their craft. He has what great entertainers have: Total concentration to be as good as he can be all of the time.

—*Johnny Mathis, singer and member at Riviera*

The L.A. Open is played every year at Riviera Country Club, which has reciprocity with Hillcrest, my home club. All it took was a phone call from my pro Jay Norman to get me on. I showed up, paid my money, and then the pro told me he wanted me to play with a member. "Devare Anderson just went off Number 1. Why don't you head out and catch him?" I did as I was told. The clubhouse and the first tee sit high above the first fairway, with a sweeping view of several holes. I hit a 240-yard tee shot and parred the two opening par 5's. On Number 3, I caught up with Devare, introduced myself, and explained my mission. We became fast friends.

Riviera was designed by George Thomas in 1927 and sits in a valley surrounded by the expensive homes of Pacific Palisades perched on the cliffs above. The grass is kikuyu, which I had never played on before. It's a very coarse grass with stiff, strong blades (so stiff that your ball sits up beautifully in the fairway, almost like it's teed up). The rough, however, tangles around your club mercilessly.

Devare and I came around the far corner to Number 6, the most famous hole on the course. It's a par 3 of 142-yards with a sand bunker right in the middle of the green—that's right, in the middle of the green! Pros have been known to chip over the trap when necessary, but the sign by the green makes clear that this is not acceptable (it digs up the green). I made a bogey here, landing my tee shot on the wrong side of the sand trap and 3-putting around the trap. Oh well! As we left the green, Devare pointed to a house high above the 6th green. "That's where I live."

Number 10, the second-most memorable hole on this course, is a 321-yard par 4, a dogleg right with lots of sand in the landing area. The sand creates an optical illusion that makes the green look more drivable than it is. I landed left of the sand, but I would guess that the expansive bunkers that sit 100 yards in front of the green catch lots of tee shots. As we walked down the 12th fairway, Devare pointed out Mel Brooks' house. Finally, we came to 18, a big dogleg right, uphill finishing par 4 that's so steep there's a periscope by the tee to see if the group in front of you is out of range. It's a hard fairway to hit and a strong finishing hole.

Riviera is not a club of celebrities like Bel-Air, but there are a few. O.J. was a member until his trial. And there's the story about Dean Martin and two of his pals getting ready to tee off when Buddy Hackett spotted them and hurried over to join them. "Sorry, Buddy," Dean said, "We already have a full threesome."

nature takes its course

BLACK DIAMOND RANCH

This will either be the best course or the worst course I have ever designed.

—*Tom Fazio, course architect*

Black Diamond Ranch was one of the early courses on my quest, yet I knew relatively little about it. With a little research I found out that it's located in Lecanto, Florida, about 90 miles north of Tampa in an area known for horse ranches. Stan Olsen, an aggressive real-estate developer, bought one of the horse ranches to build this development. He hired renowned golf architect Tom Fazio to build the course in 1988, and it was on the Top 100 as soon as it qualified. I played it shortly thereafter.

How do you get on the course? Real-estate developers want to sell houses and they know that potential buyers will want to play the golf course before they sign on the dotted line. Once again I became a home-buying prospect (fat chance at this point in my life). I was headed to Florida to promote George Winston concerts in Orlando and Tampa, so I called the sales office of Black Diamond Ranch to schedule a home tour. Of course I mentioned that I would not even consider buying unless I could play the golf course, the primary reason I would consider moving there. A few minutes later I had set up a home tour and tee time. They put me up in one of the model homes ($54 for the night) and charged me $75 for the round. Yeah, I'm on!

When I arrived at Black Diamond Ranch, I was escorted to a luxurious three-bedroom home — not bad for $54 —and taken on a real-estate tour. I was treated like royalty. After dinner in the clubhouse and a good night's sleep, I went to the driving range to meet Craig (the golf pro turned real-estate salesman) and Jack and his wife (another home-buying prospect). After a few minutes of talking to Craig, I learned that the switch from golf pro to real-estate sales was a good one. He makes more money and works fewer hours. Best of all, he plays more golf than most pros on one of the world's greatest golf courses with prospects like me.

The front nine of the course is terrific, but nothing compared to the back nine. The holes are artfully designed and the course is in fabulous condition, featuring generous, sculpted fairways. Fazio may be the best golf architect of his time. His courses are challenging for good players, yet fun for less skilled players. It's a win-win combination. Unlike most similar developments, the homes here do not encroach on the golf course, and unlike most developers, Stan Olsen maintained the natural beauty of the course's surroundings. Black Diamond also may be the first golf course built in an abandoned quarry. The five holes in the quarry have brought notoriety to Black Diamond Ranch. Tom Fazio later told me on the phone that during his first inspection of the property, Stan Olsen had not bothered to show him the quarry; it never occurred to him that it would be part of the golf course. When he finally saw it, Fazio knew the quarry would be an integral part of his plan. Suddenly, Fazio told me, other developers and golf-course architects were looking for abandoned quarries.

As we came back to the clubhouse, we encountered Number 9, a beautifully designed par 5 with a 60-foot increase in elevation from tee to green. The tee shot over water forces you to determine how much to cut off. The second shot is to a split fairway, one leading to a shorter, more demanding approach to the green than the other. But Black Diamond Ranch really begins on Number 13. The first of the five holes that play through the two rock quarries, it features vertical drops of 100 feet, large boulders, and sheer rock cliffs as a backdrop to Black Diamond Lake. On Number 17, a 200-yard par 3, Jack pulled his 3-wood tee shot so far left it should have been lost. But in this rock quarry, it hit the sheer rock cliff and careened right in front of the green, no more than 15 feet from the front pin placement. He chipped in for birdie. How lucky is that? I shot a 93, a good score for me at that time. I would love to play this place every day. In fact, I liked it so much I would rank Black Diamond in my Top 10.

LAKE NONA

The only time my prayers are never answered is playing golf.
—*Reverend Billy Graham*

Lake Nona is where famed golf instructor David Leadbetter lives and does most of his teaching. I was hoping that a trip there would improve my game. Maybe a little of Leadbetter's aura would rub off on me. No such luck.

My company made CD compilations for WLOQ in Orlando, Florida. The station is managed by John Gross, who originally is from Minneapolis, and we became friends as a result of a few years of working on CD projects together. He joined Lake Nona soon after it was built, and he was happy to host me there. I flew to Orlando and spent the night at John's house in the aquarium room—fish, bright lights, and all. I woke up the next morning to a raging thunderstorm. Lightning flashed and thunder cracked like it was hitting next door. Luckily, in this part of the country these storms move through quickly. "I'm going to work today instead, but you go ahead," John said. "I got it cleared for you." It was my first solo Top 100 experience, but it would not be my last.

The storm was winding down as I got to Lake Nona, but the course wouldn't be open for another hour-and-a-half due to the amount of rain that had fallen. I went over to the driving range. No David Leadbetter, but someone was filming a television commercial for Titleist golf balls, and half the range was taken over by serious ball strikers who where hitting balls during and between takes. Rocco Mediate and Jerry Pate were the only two in the commercial that I recognized. The range is huge and people hit from both ends. As I was taking a break and watching the commercial taping, I was hit by a golf ball in the thigh. It came from the other end (more than 300 yards away), and although it was almost completely out of energy, it was still traveling on the fly and it stung. Two nearby guys from the pro shop jumped to action; one sped to the other side of the range to see who hit it and the other rushed me to the clubhouse to get some ice. When I returned to the range, I learned it was Anders Forsbrand, then a star of the European PGA tour, who had hit the ball that hit me.

Finally, I got in a cart, which was mandatory. I rather like playing by myself occasionally. No need to be "America's Best Guest." I could stop and ponder the holes as they came up, and if I wanted to hit a few practice shots or try other tees along the way, no problem. I had time to work on my skills and practice reading the yardage to the green. Even with all that distraction, however, I was done in two-and-a-half hours.

Lake Nona was designed by Tom Fazio in 1986. It is one of his earlier works and Fazio certainly has done more masterful work since. The course is deserving of Top 100 status, although it has dropped off the list. Many tour professionals live here, including Annika Sorenstam, Ernie Els, and Sergio Garcia. A one-day event called the Tavistock Cup pits the tour pros who live at Lake Nona against the tour pros who live at Isleworth (Mark O'Meara, Tiger Woods, etc.). John and I went in 2005 and discovered that it is one of the few events where you can get anywhere near Tiger because the galleries are so small. All 12 players in the event played from 7,200 yards, and Annika beat half of them.

back to cali

PASATIEMPO GOLF CLUB

My favorite hole in all of golf is here, so much my favorite that I built my home here.

—Alister MacKenzie, course designer

In 1993, Pasatiempo was rated No. 100 on the list. Would it still be on next year, or the next? I wondered. Was it worth the chance that it might drop off? An unusual combination of public and private, it's not cheap to join but allows public play. It's located in Santa Cruz, California, about 50 miles up the coast from the more famous Pebble Beach, Spyglass, and Cypress Point. I was in the vicinity, so I decided to play it. Am I glad I did! I've been back twice and would play it again in an instant.

Alister MacKenzie designed Pasatiempo in 1929. MacKenzie also designed Cypress Point and Augusta National, as well as the Valley Club and Crystal Downs, which are on the Top 100. Holes Number 1 and 2 work their way downhill toward the Pacific, framing the ocean with Cypress trees the entire way. Annie and I enjoyed the view and loved the course.

As you walk up the 6th fairway, approximately 100 yards from the green, you see the home in which MacKenzie once lived, a fitting shrine for the world's greatest golf-course architect. Number 16 was MacKenzie's favorite hole in golf, which is saying something since he designed some of the most famous par 3's in existence. "The 16th green is a garden spot," he once said. "After playing a drive over the point of the hill, you hesitate to spoil the delightful quiet of this grassy velvet nestling in the trees. It is indeed a beautiful par 4."

None of the other courses MacKenzie designed are public. So if you get a chance to play Pasatiempo, don't hesitate!

a tree grows in toledo

INVERNESS CLUB

If profanity had any influence on the flight of the golf ball, the game would be played far better than it is.

—Horace G. Hutchinson

Sara Collins, who worked with me at SRO, has a close friend Richard Hylant in Toledo, Ohio, who is a member at Inverness. I sat next to him at her wedding, and a few weeks later I was on my way to Toledo. Inverness was founded as nine-hole course and redesigned by Donald Ross in 1919 with the purchase of additional land. George and Tom Fazio redesigned it again in 1966, adding three new holes and eliminating three others.

Inverness has hosted four U.S. Opens, two PGA Championships, and a U.S. Amateur. A few of these tournaments have brought some notoriety to the course. In 1931, Billy Burke and George Von Elm were tied at the end of regulation play. After a 36-hole playoff, they were tied again. Billy Burke won the subsequent 36-hole playoff by one stroke. It still stands as the longest playoff in the history of golf.

The 1979 U.S. Open is remembered fondly because of a tree. The 528-yard eighth hole was designed as a classic three-shot par 5, with a severe dogleg left and five deep bunkers in proximity of the green. Where others saw trouble, Lon Hinkle saw an opportunity when he discovered, during practice, that nothing prevented a player from hitting a tee shot through a narrow opening of trees onto the adjacent 17th fairway, then lofting a long second shot over trees onto the eighth green, a shortcut that cut 80 yards off the intended track.

The USGA was not thrilled about his strategy, which compromised the integrity of the three-shot hole and the safety of the gallery on the 17th hole. After Hinkle revealed his shortcut on day one, a very tall tree was planted in the middle of the night to the left of the tee box to plug the gap. Today, you can still see what is now fondly referred to as the Hinkle tree blocking the former route through the 17th fairway. The question still remains: Is it legal to alter a golf course during the course of a championship?

The 1986 PGA Championship went down in history for a different reason. The final pairing of the last day was Bob Tway and Greg Norman. Tway was four shots down at the turn, but they came to the 18th tee box tied for the lead. Tway's second shot caught the greenside bunker; Norman was on the fringe. Tway floated his ball out of that bunker right into the hole. When the cheering died down, Norman 3-putted to lose the championship by two shots.

Inverness is well designed and challenging, but I favor courses that have beauty and terrific views. Yet for its challenge alone, this course deserves its spot on the Top 100, even if it lacks the magnificence of Pebble Beach, Cypress Point, or even Black Diamond Ranch.

land of 10,000 lakes

HAZELTINE NATIONAL

INTERLACHEN COUNTRY CLUB

What other people may find in poetry or art museums, I find in the flight of a good drive.

—*Arnold Palmer*

Hazeltine and Interlachen are the two Minnesota courses on the Top 100. I have played both several times, and somehow I don't think about them as courses on my quest, but they are no less important or interesting than the others I've played.

Hazeltine is certainly the best known of the two. Named for the lake on which it sits, the course was founded in 1962 by Totton Heffelfinger, whose ultimate goal was to host a national championship in Minnesota. The course was designed by Robert Trent Jones, Sr., and hosted a U.S. Open in 1970, which brought it plenty of negative press when competitors such as Dave Hill said, "The only thing that Hazeltine is missing is 80 acres of corn and a few cows."

Avoiding further embarrassment, it was redesigned into the masterpiece for championship golf that it is known as today. Hazeltine again hosted the U.S. Open in 1991, which got lots of play in the media for two reasons: the 18-hole Monday playoff between Payne Stewart and Scott Simpson, which Stewart won; and a thunderstorm that rolled in unexpectedly on Thursday. (Six people were struck by lightning, one of whom died, by the signature 16th hole.) The course also hosted a PGA Championship in 2002; another PGA Championship is scheduled in 2009, as is the Ryder Cup in 2016.

Hazeltine is a golf-only club—no tennis, no swimming pool. Every hole is a strong test of golf. I have played it several times and have several friends who are members. My favorite holes are the holes in which water comes into play. Number 7 is a par 5 with a pond fronting the green. Number 8, is a beautiful par 3 with water on both the front and right side of the green. The 10th and 16th greens both jut out into Lake Hazeltine. Number 10 is a severe dogleg left that tumbles down the hill to a green that sits on the lake. Number 16 is the signature hole, formerly a par 3, now converted to a par 4, with the green sitting on its own peninsula on Lake Hazeltine.

Interlachen, in the suburb of Edina, is my favorite course in Minnesota, but I don't get to play here as often as I would like. Although I know several members, invitations are rare. The setting is very serene: beautiful rolling hills, lovely lakes and ponds, many of which are framed by lush weeping willows. It's a Donald Ross design and by far one of his better ones, with plenty of elevation changes and lots of water that comes into play.

In 1930, Interlachen hosted a U.S. Open, the third of Bobby Jones' grand-slam victories that year, when he skipped his ball over the water onto the 18th green for a spectacular finish. A few months later, he won the U.S. Amateur at Merion to win an unprecedented grand slam. In 2008, Interlachen will host the U.S. Women's Open.

Several years ago, a friend of mine was married at Interlachen and the ceremony was held on the 18th green. Annie and I were at Turnberry in Scotland at the time, so I gave a golf ball with a Turnberry logo to a friend who rolled it across the green immediately after the ceremony, then read a message from us: "In honor of today's wedding, we hit this ball across the Atlantic Ocean in hopes that it reaches you on the 18th green at Interlachen. Congratulations on your wedding."

forest gump-tion

FOREST HIGHLANDS

Practice puts brains in your muscles.

—Sam Snead

When most people think of Arizona golf courses, they think of the desert courses of Tucson and Phoenix. But Flagstaff, two hours north of Phoenix in a completely different climate, is home to what may be the best golf course in the state, Forest Highlands. A friend of a friend told me he had worked in the pro shop there a couple of years ago and would call the head pro for me. After two or three follow-up calls brought no action, I decided to take matters into my own hands. "Hi, my name is Larry Berle, and Billy Johnson, who used to work there, told me to call you." "Oh, yeah," he said. "How's Billy doing?" "Fine," I said and mentioned the city he was living in (which was the only thing I knew about him). Fortunately, the head pro did not ask any more questions about Billy. "When do you want to come out?" he asked. I was not only on, but I would be playing for free. I called my father-in-law, Terry O'Brien, who lived in Phoenix, and a week later we were off to Flagstaff. I filled Terry in on my "relationship" with Billy so he would not spoil our cover. We were on the tee sheet, but the head pro was not around, so I escaped disaster.

Forest Highlands could easily make my Top 10 list. Designed by Tom Weiskopf and Jay Morrish, the property is nestled in among tall pine trees that frame the snowcapped San Francisco Peaks in the distance. Elevation changes abound at Forest Highlands, and many of the holes play downhill through those towering pines. The course is only open in the summer, and we were blessed with a perfect day. Both Terry and I were blown away by this golf experience.

With this round at Forest Highlands, I'd played 22 courses on my quest. I'd picked off the easy ones, courses for which I had clear connections and courses that allowed public access. If I hoped to achieve my goal of playing the Top 100, I would have to get serious about how to accomplish it. If my experiences so far had taught me anything, it was that the best way to do that was to expand the network of people who could help me. Why would complete strangers help me on my quest? I didn't have an answer for that. All I knew was that it had happened, and I started developing a strategy to expand my network.

The first thing I did was to begin writing a newsletter every three or four months, and send it to those who had helped me or expressed some interest in following my quest. The newsletter had several purposes. I liked to write, and it was a good way to chronicle my experiences. I wanted to share these experiences with my circle of friends and get their feedback (especially when they said they wished they were in my shoes and encouraged me to keep going). And most of all, I wanted to expand my network, so I closed each letter with a note about four or five courses that I wanted to play next, hoping to find someone with that elusive connection.

Keep in mind that this was 1993—before blogging, even before email—so sending out a newsletter meant writing, Xeroxing, printing mailing labels, stamping, and stuffing and sealing envelopes. It was an experiment that as time went on proved very effective. I eventually had about a hundred readers. Everyone I knew could read about my progress and be reminded of my quest. You'd be surprised how often somebody knew someone who could help me. The next three courses turned out to be easy to get on. They were all resorts in Hawaii and open to the public.

aloha

PRINCE COURSE

In all the world, I never expect to find a more spectacularly beautiful place to build a golf course than Princeville overlooking Hanalei Bay.

—*Robert Trent Jones, Jr., golf-course designer*

Annie and I traveled to Hawaii in the winter of 1994. Hawaii has three golf courses on the Top 100 and we intended to play them all. First stop was the island of Kauai, home to the Prince Course and Kauai Lagoons. Evidence of the typhoon a few years earlier was still in places along the coast, where several hotels were washed into the sea. Fortunately, Princeville Resort, on the north end of the island, had survived. The resort was luxurious and the golf course was like walking through a painting of a rain forest, with an emerald path cut down the center. It climbs, slopes, and careens up and down hills. The fairways looked generous, until the wind got a hold of a stray shot and suddenly they seemed as narrow as bowling alleys. The trade winds blow constantly. The course is named for Prince Albert, son of King Kamehameha IV, former king of Hawaii.

Four holes were particularly memorable. Number 1 is in Golf Digest's Top 10 starting holes and may be the toughest opening hole I have ever played. Not a very friendly welcome to the course—but it just kept getting better. Number 7 on the front nine is a par 3 sitting right on a 300-foot cliff over the Pacific Ocean and one of the windiest places I ever have tried to hit a golf ball. Number 12 tees off from a cliff a hundred feet above the fairway. You stand above the treetops, with rain forest on three sides of you and a lush green strip of fairway in front of you. A well-struck tee shot has a hang time that any NFL punter would die for. Number 13 has the opposite effect. At the end of this par 5, you face a green cut into an amphitheater with a 180-degree, 75-foot-high wall of rain forest surrounding you. At the back is a waterfall pouring into a small creek. Simply breathtaking!

A few months later, my friend Josh Levenson was headed to Kauai on vacation. As I described the beauty of this course to him, I could tell it wasn't really registering because he isn't a golfer. We had done a lot of running together, so I told him he should run the cart path of the course. He called me from the hotel to tell me he had run the course at sunrise and how beautiful it was, and he thanked me profusely for suggesting it. There is more than one way to appreciate golf architecture.

KAUAI LAGOONS

We share a love for the unrelenting challenge of golf. It's this challenge—on every level—that keeps us from walking away from this game. The fact is that humans like to be challenged. And in golf, every shot is a challenge. Every shot.

—Andy Mill, former Olympic skier

Kauai Lagoons, about 50 miles down the coast from Princeville, is home to a hotel and two wonderful golf courses designed by Jack Nicklaus. When we were there in 1994, the hotel was closed and being refurbished after it had been devastated by a typhoon, but the golf courses seemed to have come through unscathed. It felt a bit like being in ghost town, but the course was worth it.

Forty acres of fresh-water lagoons run throughout the property and boats take guests from one area to another. The hotel has since been restored to its former glory and is now run by Marriott. The fairways weave along imposing ocean cliffs and some are truly spectacular. One of the holes (certainly not the best) shares a fence line with the Kauai airport. If a plane buzzing your head doesn't affect your swing, it's not so bad. But there was a moment that I felt sure that I could have hit a plane coming in for a landing if I had teed off.

A little cupola of a building sits on a small island in one of the lagoons near the 17th tee. I inquired about it and discovered that it's a small wedding chapel. Each tee box has a white marble statue welcoming you to the hole featuring such images as a Happy Buddha, an elephant and, of course, on 18, a golden bear. With the hotel fully operational now, I have no doubt this is a magnificent place.

MAUNA KEA

Mauna Kea Golf Course has the best set of par 3s of any course in Hawaii. Each is unique in its character, aesthetics, and shot value.

—*Mark Rolfing, NBC golf analyst*

Annie and I flew to the Big Island of Hawaii to play Mauna Kea, the last of Hawaii's Top 100 golf courses we played on this trip. Mauna Kea is a luxurious resort that sits on the western coast of the island. It was developed by Laurance Rockefeller more than 40 years ago on a large field of black lava. In December 1964, he brought in renowned golf architect Robert Trent Jones, Sr., father of the designer of the Prince course, who knew just by looking at it that he could grow grass on the lava field. The dramatic play of the sea and lava is remarkable.

The course sits on a crescent-shaped beach where the pure white sand meets the shimmering aqua water. It has dramatic elevation changes, with panoramic views of the Pacific Ocean and the snow-capped Mauna Kea mountain peak that towers over the island. Sixteen of the 18 holes play inland, but the two ocean-side holes are spectacular. Mauna Kea has a terrific collection of par 3s. Our favorite was Number 3, a 200-yard hole starting from a cliffside tee above a raging ocean inlet in which surging water races to meet the rocky, lava-strewn shoreline. Number 11 is just as spectacular. The view from the tee, which sits some 100 feet above the green, is breathtaking with the Pacific Ocean as its backdrop.

a golfer's dream

tennessee torture

THE HONORS COURSE

I have never been uncomfortable performing with my guitar, but in golf (especially on the first tee), I feel: Okay, Mr. Should Have Been a Pro Golfer, let's see what you can do.

—Vince Gill, country music star and scratch handicap

In the fall of 1994, I was promoting several dates on the Yanni tour. For those of you who know who he is, he needs no explanation. For those of you who don't, Yanni is a stunningly handsome Greek new-age musician with enormous ambition toward stardom. Linda Evans (of Dynasty fame) heard Yanni's music and called his record company to ask how to reach him. She wanted to let him know how much she loved his music. Their very public romance skyrocketed Yanni's career, and their appearance together on Oprah sold tens of thousands of albums. In a brilliant marketing move, Yanni gave his video performance Live at the Acropolis to public TV stations across the country to air during pledge weeks and gave his CDs as premium gifts to donating viewers, a strategy that has been copied many times and did wonders for his sales. Getting permission to perform at the Acropolis was no easy feat. Two weeks before the concert, the orchestra that he had contracted backed out. He went deep into his own pocketbook to hire a replacement orchestra and fly its musicians to Athens from London, a high-risk move that ended up paying a high reward.

Yanni originally is from Minneapolis, and I had been involved in promoting his concerts from the time of his first record. As his star shone more brightly, I was promoting dates in 8,000- to 10,000-

seat amphitheaters in several cities across the United States. It was lucrative enough for me that my wife calls our home "the house that Yanni built." One of those concerts was in Nashville. The Honors Course is about a hundred miles from Nashville in a tiny bedroom community outside of Chattanooga called Ooltewah. I called the head pro, explained my quest, and said I was promoting a concert with Yanni in Nashville. I offered him tickets for anyone there, if I could just have the honor (get it?) of playing the Honors Course. Now Yanni is not usually the type of performer who is likely to appeal to golf pros, but they do have girlfriends, who might be more impressed by an invitation to see him. "Okay," he said, "be here Thursday around 11." I arranged to fly to Nashville one day early and drive down to the Honors Course.

I got in Wednesday night and drove toward Chattanooga. About 30 miles from the course, I found a good motel and decided to drive the last 45 minutes the next morning. I woke up early and was on the road with plenty of time to spare. About 10 miles before Chattanooga I passed a sign reading: "Now Entering Eastern Time Zone." Tennessee is split into two time zones, a fact that had escaped me, and now I was going to be a half-hour late. Luckily, it wasn't a problem.

You'll never find the Honors Course without specific directions—go past the third light, and when you see the large propane tank on the right, quickly look left and you'll see the entrance road—but I found it just as the head pro had described it to me: a small road leading to a wooden split-rail gate with a speaker box on it. The Honors Course sign was so small you had to look twice to see it. Why didn't they just put up a big "Go away!" sign. I pressed the button, and someone in the pro shop acknowledged me and buzzed me in. Late, shmate. There are no tee times at the Honors Course. A big day is 10 foursomes (the typical public course can host that number in less than two hours), so it's just show up and play.

No one can play the Honors Course without a member or at least someone from the pro shop. I was paired with an assistant pro named Dave for the first 12 holes. He had a hot date that night and had to leave, so on the 13th tee box, a female assistant pro came out to complete the round with me. The course was designed by Pete "golfers love torture, that's where I come in" Dye in 1983. It is 7,000 yards from the tips and has a rating of 75.4 and a slope of 151. To the best of my knowledge, 151 is the highest slope that USGA has given out, and this course is as challenging as it gets. This little hideaway, which sits in a valley at the foot of White Oak Mountain, was the brainchild of Coca-Cola magnate Jack Lupton, who wanted to honor the amateur golfer and create an indelible impression on each and every player; I would say he succeeded. The only thing missing from the course is railroad ties, one of Pete Dye's "trademarks," because Lupton didn't want any, but even that omission doesn't make it any easier. Among all this difficulty I did find one rather fun element: the "echo bunker." If you speak into the bunker behind the 6th green, it echoes back to you, which is not such a good thing if you are swearing a blue streak after a bad sand shot. I had a lovely afternoon with my two pros as we wound our way through the 18 holes set in 460 acres of the heavily wooded Tennessee hills.

The following year, the Honors Course hosted the Curtis Cup, and I was able to watch the greatest female amateur golfers of the world on television as they struggled with the course. "Yes, it's not just me," I thought. Pete Dye tells a couple of funny stories in his book about the construction of the Honors Course. In the first one, Jack, Pete, and Pete's wife, Alice, were standing on the 10th tee when Alice said, "This fairway won't do at all. It needs to be low-ered 10 feet." The crew dug down two feet and hit limestone. Three hundred thousand dollars later, Jack jokingly told Alice to leave the premises and never come back. Then there was the question of the grass type: Jack wanted Bermuda; Pete wanted Zoysia. Jack won (he was paying the bills), but, unbeknownst to Jack, a patch of Zoysia was planted on the approach to the 6th green. Winter-kill took its toll on the Bermuda, but the Zoysia kept on growing. Jack called Pete: "I want Zoysia on my golf course." He repeated it a few times quite clearly, until Pete got the message that he meant now. Within a week Jack had his fairways resodded with Zoysia. Just imagine how much it costs and how long it takes to sod an entire golf course!

wichita fly-in

PRAIRIE DUNES

A touch of Scotland in the Land of Oz. Sunflowers instead of heather. Oceans of grain instead of sea. But like Scotland, be prepared. The wind always blows.

—*Tom Watson, honorary member of Prairie Dunes*

Later in the fall of 1994, the pro at Hillcrest, Jay Norman, called Prairie Dunes to see if I would be allowed to play. The answer was yes. In Wichita, Kansas, I had recently met Randy Henwood, who had always wanted to play Prairie Dunes and had an airplane. He had the plane and I had the permission to play Prairie Dunes, so we had a match. I flew commercial jet to Kansas City, and Randy picked me up in his plane and we flew to Hutchinson, Kansas. Aside from my training as a glider pilot, this was the first time I had ever been in a private small airplane. The views as you fly over Kansas are not compelling, but flying in a single-engine private plane to play golf—now that's a thrill! Why a private plane? If you look on a map you'll see that Hutchinson, Kansas, is in the middle of nowhere.

We scoped out the golf course as we came in for a landing at the Hutchinson Airport. The airport operators gave us a courtesy car (how great is that?) and a two-mile drive later we arrived at Prairie Dunes. It was windy as hell when we landed, and even windier when we played golf. The wind was clocked at 25 mph at the airport, and it was gusting higher than that at the course. When we arrived, the flags flying above the clubhouse were stiff as cardboard.

Prairie Dunes, designed by Perry Maxwell in 1937, is a Scottish style course with hardly any trees and lots of trouble. God forbid they should put up a few trees to protect you from the wind. There are basically two velocities of wind here: windy and windier. On that rare occasion of calm, this would not be a very difficult golf course, so how difficult with wind, you ask? Jack Nicklaus, in eight appearances here, never broke par. Sam Sneed, after his first look at the narrow fairway on Number 1, turned to the gallery and said, "Okay, folks, we'll have to walk single file today."

I bogeyed Number 1 and made a 60-foot putt for par on Number 2. Number 8 was picked by Sports Illustrated for its "Best 18 Holes in America." I got a double bogey. On Number 9, Jack Nicklaus once scored an 8, and I actually beat Jack Nicklaus on that hole. Wait till I tell him. Number 11 is a 442-yard downwind par 4. I am not a big hitter, but I was a 9-iron away. According to the yardage book, "The approach shot must negotiate a knob in front of the green that is specifically designed to prevent roll-up shots." I hit my 9-iron high and short in front of that knob. The wind was so strong that my ball went up and over that knob onto and off of the back of the green. Now that's windy.

The wind finally calmed down as we rode back to the airpark in our courtesy car and took off into the sunset, heading for Randy's home in Wichita. I was exhausted from fighting the wind all day. I'm still not sure how Randy stayed alert enough to fly home, but thank God he did.

struck by the stick

CROOKED STICK

When Mark O'Meara first stepped on the 13th tee during the practice round for the 1991 PGA Championship at Crooked Stick, he took one look at the pin placement and yelled over to me, "Oh I see, Pete, a dogleg par 3."

—Pete Dye, course designer

How on earth did they come up with this name for a golf course? As Pete Dye tells it in his book, Bury Me in a Pot Bunker, he was walking the unfinished back nine when he picked up a knobby, crooked stick to swat a stone and charter member Bill Wick, who was walking with him, suggested the name. It stuck.

The only time I had heard about Crooked Stick was when John Daly came out of nowhere to win the PGA Championship there in 1991. When I read Pete's book, I learned of the enormous attention that event brought to the course. To protect the course against long hitters, Pete had built slight inclines into the fairway landing areas to impede forward roll. John Daly flew right over those landing areas, hitting it so long that most of the hazards were not even in play. "Over four days, John Daly demolished my golf course! He drove the ball where no man had ever driven it before," Pete Dye wrote. A fact that adds to the Cinderella story: If Nick Price hadn't withdrawn at the last minute, John Daly, who was an alternate in the field, would have never played in the tournament that catapulted him into golf limelight.

My friend Michael Lach lives in Carmel, California, but spent most of his life in Indianapolis. His former brother-in-law is a member at Crooked Stick, and he said he would arrange for me to play. He placed the call and paved the way for me to arrange things. A few weeks later, I was promoting a Sinbad concert in Indianapolis, so we set the date. Three days before the scheduled date, my host (who shall remain nameless) called to say that something had come up and he would be unavailable to play that day. He did not offer an alternative, so I hung up the phone a very disappointed golfer. Then a light bulb went off in my head. Golf pros love comedy. I'll call the pro shop and offer to trade some tickets to Sinbad for an opportunity to play golf. "Bingo!" They went for it, and I was on.

I arrived the day before the concert to some heavy rain, but it cleared up around dawn, and by 8:30 a.m., I was at the course. It was not raining, but it was very wet. The parking lot was almost empty. I went into the pro shop, introduced myself, and they said I was welcome to go play by myself. I told them about my "host" who had backed out of playing with me, and the pro said, "Mr. Nameless Host is in the dining room having breakfast." He and his companion were the only two people there aside from me and the shop staff. Imagine his surprise when I walked into the dining room and introduced myself. I was polite, but I would love to know what he was thinking when I introduced myself.

It was my second experience playing a Top 100 course alone in wet conditions, but it was wonderful. Every putt left a trail on the green, and I took this opportunity to practice green reading. When I missed putts, I went back and putted again, with the dew trails teaching me their mysterious lessons. The overcast sky and mist-filled atmosphere made it feel like I was playing in a dream. I encountered Pete Dye's famous railroad ties and something I hadn't seen before, his equally famous bridges over streams made from railroad boxcars—very cool. I discovered that Mr. Dye lives in a house near the 18th green. On the opposite side of the fairway from his house was a pond that hugged the entire right side of this dogleg.

In the middle of that pond was an island of no more than 50 square feet. On that island was a mailbox with a sign on it: "Club

Suggestion Box." Are you supposed to swim to it with your written suggestion clutched in your teeth? I laughed myself silly.

Pete and Alice Dye raised the money themselves to develop Crooked Stick in 1964. At the time they had several other inconsequential designs under their belt, but Pete calls Crooked Stick his firstborn because it was the first course in which he was involved in every detail. He obviously was a natural talent, because he sure mastered his craft quickly. In Bury Me in a Pot Bunker, Dye describes some of the elements that he used in creating Crooked Stick. He speaks at length of the variety of holes and the shots they demand, holes that dogleg left and right; holes of every direction so the golfer has to face downwind, upwind, and crosswind; easy holes followed by harder holes followed by easier holes; positioning hazards primarily right on one hole and left on the next; and a particularly challenging final three holes, just to challenge a golfer's mental stamina as he finishes the round. All of these are elements that most golfers would agree make a great golf course. Crooked Stick is where Dye began experimenting with the creation of dips, swales, hollows, and undulations throughout the fairways and greens. He also notes an interesting illusion that he created "where the golfers appear to be playing down toward an illusionary elevated green. Most of the greens are really at ground level, but with so much earth removed in front, they appear elevated in the mind's eye." There is a saying among the members: "Sooner or later the Stick will get you."

After lunch I headed to the theater for sound check and told Sinbad about my day, but he topped me. He had spent the afternoon visiting Mike Tyson, who was in prison just outside of Indianapolis for sexual assault. Guess who got Sinbad's limo bill?

Crooked Stick will host the U.S. Senior Men's Open in 2009. Watch for it on TV.

a golfer's dream

flowers in the desert

DESERT HIGHLANDS

This is a golf course that is unique among any of the courses I've been involved with. Desert Highlands begins with probably a greater and denser variety of desert foliage than I've ever seen. Added to this are the rocks of Pinnacle Peak and the views, which are outstanding. The course is built with a concept of harmonizing the course and the desert vegetation in a design format not used to this extreme before. The average golfer must become a more intelligent player to challenge the course successfully.

—Jack Nicklaus, course designer

In 1994 and 1995, I had a contract with the Phoenix Symphony Orchestra to help them produce pops concerts. The director of marketing at the symphony was Joan Laskey. One day in a meeting, I happened to mention that I was working on playing the Top 100, and Desert Highlands was on the list (as was Desert Forest, Desert Mountain, and Troon Country Club). I was hoping that they had someone on their board of directors who was a member at one of these exclusive places, but I guess avid golfers rarely become members of symphony-orchestra boards. However, Joan had a cousin at Desert Highlands, Marty Boxer, and she called him. "I would love to host him," Marty said. A couple of days later, I was teeing it up at Desert Highlands with Marty and a guy from Iowa named John Holz.

Desert Highlands is located in northern Scottsdale in a gated community. It sits several hundred feet in elevation above the Phoenix Valley floor with breathtaking views of Phoenix, Pinnacle Peak, and the surrounding mountains. The clubhouse is built with a very low profile so you can barely see it when you approach. Great lengths have been taken to blend the environment and the development. The course has received many accolades and hosted the inaugural Skins game in 1984 with Jack Nicklaus, Tom Watson, Gary Player, and Arnold Palmer.

Marry and I hit it off immediately. We hit balls at the driving range and practiced in the short-game area, before he took me to the 18-hole putting course a few hundred yards away. I have never seen anything like this at a golf course; it is certainly not to be confused with a miniature golf course. The putting course is a series of four greens with a total of 18 holes, nine out and nine back. They are fast, severe greens, and although I have now played the putting course several times, I've never even come close to scoring par 36. And putting is a pretty strong suite of mine.

The first tee sits on a rock cliff 125 feet above the fairway, with boulder-sided mountains hugging the right side of the fairway. Even though it's a 360-yard hole, everyone hits a 5- or 6-iron off the tee to the middle of the fairway. It's easy to get caught up in the beauty and miss an easy scoring opportunity here. After that comes ample but undulating fairways with desert left and right and many forced carries over desert washes. Number 6 is called gambler's choice with one of Nicklaus' famous split fairways: safe on one side, riskier on the other but with the promise of an easier shot to the green. Number 14 approaches Pinnacle Peak, and on number 15, a short par 3, Pinnacle Peak shoves a rocky shoulder into the green. Number 16 turns its back on Pinnacle Peak and gives the golfer a sweeping view of the valley below.

Jack Nicklaus has had a long and varied career as a golf architect. Desert Highlands was built during what I call his "penal period" of trying to make courses as hard as possible. With undulating greens, many forced carries, and the desert always looming close on the sides of the fairways, he was successful. The card shows it with a rating of 73.9 and a slope of 151.

Marty Boxer and I became fast friends, and we continue to see each other when I am in Phoenix. One year when we got together his right arm was in a sling. "No golf for a few weeks for me," he said. He explained that he had been driving his golf cart from the edge of the fairway over a mound, caught his wheel in a fairway bunker, and rolled the cart. A few years later Marty and I went to the Masters together. Unfortunately, when he left for New Zealand to practice medicine, he resigned his membership at Desert Highlands. Fortunately, another friend of mine from Minneapolis built a house there and joined Desert Highlands, so I can play there whenever I want.

DESERT FOREST

A revolutionary landmark in golf architecture.
—*Brad Klein, Golfweek Senior Editor*

Desert Forest Golf Club in Carefree, Arizona, is widely considered the first desert-style course built. That was just the beginning of the considerable acclaim accorded to this desert gem over its 40-plus-year history. In 1962, architect Robert "Red" Lawrence carved the course from existing desert landscape, with virtually no soil having been removed or shaped during course construction. It sits at 2,500 feet of elevation, so it gets cooler weather than Phoenix and can have plenty of bad weather in winter.

The first time I played Desert Forest, it began hailing after eight holes and that was that. The following week, my host had me back, but I never got out of the clubhouse because it was cold and rainy. Three years later, I got another chance when John Stringer, a friend from Minneapolis, said, "My father-in-law is a member at Desert Forest." So I finally got my round in. John's father-in-law, Ed Morgan, was the mayor of Cave Creek, so I met everyone we ran into that day, and they were all impressed with the fact that the mayor was playing with someone who was on a quest to play the Top 100. The mayor apologized for the course because, for the past few seasons, the fairways had not been overseeded in the winter, so it was brown. It played fine, but its appearance was a hot debate point among the members. Its a bit strange to hear your playing partner say, "Good shot, you're in the brown stuff." This is one of the few clubs in Arizona that is not a real-estate development, so each hole is not surrounded by homes. It's golf-only, no swimming pool or other activities. Members' average age is 66 years old, and the course gets only about 17,000 rounds a year. The greens may be the fastest in the Phoenix area, and many people think it has the best greens in Arizona.

pennsylvania pride & prejudice

The greens are like trying to putt down a marble staircase and stop it on the third step.

—Anonymous

OAKMONT

In the early summer of 1995, Billy Weisman and Robbie Soskin (brother of Ron, whom I mentioned earlier) asked me over lunch how they could help with my quest. Now that was a switch—someone asking how they can help me! I gave them the names of some courses that I needed help to play, and Billy said, "We have a strong business relationship with a member at Oakmont." I was going to be near there later that summer to present another Yanni concert, so I was in. It turns out the host couldn't play with me that day, so I played with the assistant pro.

I played Oakmont to complete the Top 100, but I have no desire to go back. I can't understand why anyone other than the best of golfers who really enjoy being tested would want to join Oakmont. In my opinion, this collection of 18 holes is more like a penal colony than a golf course.

Oakmont was founded and designed in 1903 by Henry Fownes and his son William. Their goal was to build the most difficult golf course possible, and they succeeded. After the course was built, the Fownes boys would watch golfers play the course, and whenever they saw a player hit over a fairway bunker or hit a poor shot that went unpunished, they would instruct the greens keeper to excavate another bunker. At one time, they had directed the installation of more than 350 bunkers. The Fownes' design philosophy was that "a shot poorly played should be a shot irrevocably lost." The golf world should be damn glad that this was only course they designed.

Nearly half of the 350 bunkers disappeared over the years, filled in after William Fownes relented under pressure from the members, but 180 remain, some of them golf landmarks. The "Church Pews" bunker between the third and fourth fairways is the most famous hazard at Oakmont. It's a massive expanse of sand wasteland about the size of a football field containing eight rows of grass that will catch pulled or hooked drives from either tee.

Have I mentioned the rough yet? It may not be the longest rough I have ever played, but it certainly is the thickest and gnarliest. My club kept getting twisted up in it. (You're right: What the hell was I doing there in the first place?) How about the greens? Even the Oakmont website boasts, "Oakmont's greens are the hardest and fastest in championship golf. They were built on a base of only six inches of topsoil over a foundation of clay. The greens have always had the reputation as the fastest greens in creation." I couldn't agree more. The pro never shot at the flag, but he knew where to land the ball (often not on the green at all) to get it to end up somewhere in the vicinity of the flag. He shot a very impressive 75 that day. As I was struggling in the rough, he said that a couple of weeks before the most recent U.S. Open that had been played at Oakmont, most members were throwing their clubs down and coming in because the rough was just too much to take.

The U.S. Open returned to Oakmont in 2007. The USGA announced that a new back tee on the eighth hole will make it 285 yards long, the longest par 3 in the United States. In 2005, almost 90 players on the PGA tour failed to average 285 yards off the tee. Controversy is inevitable.

MERION

Golf and sex are the only things you can enjoy without being very good at either one of them.

—*Jimmy Demaret*

I went from a bad day of golf to a glorious one when I flew to Philadelphia the day after Oakmont. My cousin Andy Kneeter, who works in financial services in the Philadelphia area, had called: "A good friend of mine Barclay Douglas lives in Philadelphia and his neighbor Mike Talent is willing to host all three of us at Merion." I didn't know much about Merion, but I knew it was on my list. I was thrilled.

Merion Golf Club has two courses: the west course and the more famous east course. Club members sent architect Hugh Wilson to Scotland to study the best courses. He came back and fitted the holes onto the land as compactly as a jigsaw puzzle. Merion East opened in 1912. Hugh Wilson also brought back the idea of wicker baskets atop the pins, rather than flags. No one knows where this idea originated, but if you're accustomed to looking at flags for some indication of the wind direction or speed, it's not possible at Merion.

Merion is not the longest course; in fact, many say it will never hold another major championship because it's not long enough. But there should be a way to utilize this fine course for national competitions. It has hosted more national championships than any other course in the U.S. and tests every shot in the bag. I got a par on Number 11, the hole where Bobby Jones shut out his opponent in the 1930 U.S. Amateur to win the Grand Slam.

The green at Number 12 has an interesting story as well. During the 1934 U.S. Open, Walter Hagen was on the front of the green, which is sloped from front to back with a steep drop-off behind the green leading to Ardmore Avenue just beyond the back edge. The pin was in the very back. Hagen putted it long, over the edge and (you guessed it) out of bounds. Putting a ball out of bounds is embarrassing enough, so it must have been devastating to do it in front of a large gallery. Merion is also the course where Ben Hogan struggled to win the 1950 U.S. Open just 16 months after a near-fatal car crash. He played in enormous pain with both legs and ankles completely taped up. You may have seen the famous picture of Hogan, as he completes a 1-iron shot. That photo was taken on the 18th fairway of Merion.

Number 1's tee box is so close to the outdoor dining-room patio that you feel like you have to watch your follow through so as not to hit anyone with your club. Number 3 is a long par 3, a terrific reproduction of a redan hole. A stream runs through the property and Hugh Wilson makes excellent strategic use of it. It comes into play in the darndest places. Back by the clubhouse, Number 13 is a 120-yard par 3. That seems short, especially for a championship course, but it requires a deadly accurate tee shot.

Numbers 16 and 17 play across an old limestone quarry (it may have been the first course ever to do so), and of course the fantastic 18th returns to the clubhouse. You want to turn around and play it again.

I have only played Merion once, and I hope to play it again some day. If I could play only a handful of places in the world for the rest of my life, Merion would be one of them. In fact, I have told many people that if I had to choose two courses to play the rest of my life one would be Merion and the other would be Cypress Point. Merion was the birthplace of my friendship with Barclay Douglas. Barclay was captivated with my quest and we became friends. We have played several Top 100 courses together. Glory be! The USGA awarded the 2013 US Open to Merion.

l.a. confidential

LOS ANGELES COUNTRY CLUB, NORTH COURSE

I wouldn't want to join any club that would have me as a member.

—Groucho Marx

LACC has been an elusive place for me to get on. I know several people in Los Angeles, many who have powerful jobs in the music business, but I had trouble finding a way onto this course. I met Clint Mitchell when I was promoting George Winston concerts in 20 to 25 cities each year. He was promoting George Winston dates as well. A few years later he was offered a job as an agent at William Morris Agency, and occasionally we would play golf together in L.A. One day Clint said that a stockbroker he worked with was a member at LACC, and he would see if he could get us an invitation. He had never played there either, so I think this was additional motivation on his part. He called Joe Bergin and got us invited along with one of the VPs at William Morris. Suddenly, I was fulfilling my goal of playing a Top 100 course and spending four hours with a major force at William Morris that might develop into a helpful relationship in the future. You can see most of the golf course of LACC from the 18th-floor window of the William Morris Agency, which is just across the street in Century City.

I soon found out why everyone wanted to play LACC. I can't say the club is exclusionary, but there are no Jewish members, and as far as I can tell, there are no members in show business (music or film). In L.A., that leaves out many very wealthy people. Rumor has it that they don't want high-profile members who may bring unwanted attention to the club, so they don't invite them to join.

That had something to do with why these agents were so eager to get on there as well. According to GolfClubAtlas.com, the USGA aggressively pursued LACC to host a U.S. Open all through the 1980s and were refused.

LACC sits on a very expensive piece of real estate—it wouldn't surprise me if its land is the most valuable of any golf course in the U.S. It is surrounded by Century City, Beverly Hills, and Holmby Hills. Its address is 10101 Wilshire Boulevard. To those who know their way around L.A., that says it all. But as soon as you pull into the club, the hustle and bustle of L.A. quickly disappears.

Two interesting details about LACC: We walked and took caddies. At the 4th hole, the caddie said, "See that wall? That's the backyard wall to the Playboy Mansion." Even I thought about boosting myself up on that wall to see what eye candy might lie on the other side, but it was a bit high for that, and the caddie said the wall has electric wires on the top. Once, as a practical joke, they convinced a new caddie to let them give him a boost to look over the wall. When his hand reached the top, he got a big shock and was pissed at those guys for the rest of the day.

Near Number 14 (a par 5 of 528 yards) was the home of famous TV producer Aaron Spelling. It ran the length of the fairway (more than 500 yards), and makes the LACC clubhouse look like a guesthouse.

Throughout my quest, I had been taking pictures and collecting scorecards. A few weeks after I played LACC, I decided to collect a logo golf ball from every course, so I sent a self-addressed stamped padded envelope and a $5 bill to each club, with a letter asking them to send me a ball. I needed about 15 of them to complete my collection. They all sent a golf ball. A couple sent my change with the ball. One sent my $5 back. I got a note—and no ball—from the LACC: "We cannot accept cash in the pro shop. Here is your money back." I understand rules, but certainly one of the pros must have had a logo ball in his bag, or they could have asked a member to buy it and given that member the $5. So I called my host, Joe, and asked him for a ball, which he sent. I think he was embarrassed by his club's behavior. Even though LACC wouldn't take Groucho if he were alive today, I doubt that he would be interested in joining the club anyway.

a golfer's dream

on, wisconsin

BLACK WOLF RUN

The ardent golfer would play Mount Everest if somebody would put a flagstick on top.

—*Pete Dye, course architect*

When I started this quest, Wisconsin had two courses in the Top 100: the River Course at Black Wolf Run, and Milwaukee Country Club. My buddy Don Knutson and I were out running one morning (we ran together three times a week for several years) with Judy Karwosky, a woman from Madison, Wisconsin, who was staying with Don and his wife. He began boasting to her about my quest to play the Top 100. "Is the Milwaukee Country Club on that list?" Judy asked. "I know someone who is a huge golf fanatic and is a member at Milwaukee Country Club. I'm sure he would gladly host you." A few days later, she called MCC member Bob Milbourne, and sure enough, he was enthusiastic about hosting me.

I called Bob, introduced myself, and set a date. Then I called to make a reservation to play the River Course at Black Wolf Run the day before MCC. Annie and I checked into the elegant American Club, at Black Wolf Run, in Kohler, Wisconsin, and headed out to play the River Course.

If you've never been to Kohler to play golf, you must go. In the late-'80s, Herb Kohler decided he needed a golf course and hired Pete Dye to design it; he named it Black Wolf Run, in honor of the chief of the local Winnebago tribe. Kohler has four courses now and all of them are terrific, as is the American Club, the only five-diamond resort in the Midwest. The town also is the home of the plumbing-fixture dynasty Kohler, whose showroom alone is worth the trip.

It was a beautiful fall day, and our package included a short lesson from the pro, unlimited range balls, and a round of golf. The River Course is magnificent and difficult. Pete Dye really did once say, "Golfers love punishment. That's where I come in." Black Wolf Run opened for play in June 1988 and was named that year's "Best New Public Course" by Golf Digest. Scores of pot bunkers and water areas shored with railroad ties complement the Scottish influences in Dye's work. Vast undulating greens further define his vision for Black Wolf Run. Hybrid grasses delineate various sections of the course. The River Course has the Sheboygan River curling through it. In September 1986 in the midst of its construction, Mother Nature dumped eight inches of rain on the Black Wolf Run site in four hours. The torrential downpour washed out greens, irrigation pipes, and drain tiles. Everyone was devastated, but went back to work and finished this wonderful test of golf.

I loved the River Course, but I walked away thinking, why would they make a resort course so difficult? Most people see it once or twice in their lives. They don't want to lose lots of balls and they don't want the round to take forever. If I were the developer, I would make it more forgiving and enjoyable for the average player who has never seen it before. In Bury Me in a Pot Bunker, Pete Dye seems to have agreed with me. Herb Kohler really wanted a variety of high wild grasses along the fairways creating the same look of the whin and heather of Scottish links. Pete did everything he could to dissuade Herb, arguing that golfers would spend all their time looking for balls in the high grass. "My skepticism that public golfers would dread playing a course that featured such conditions was, as Herb continued to remind me, dead wrong," Pete writes. I guess I was wrong too. Another fun fact about Black Wolf Run: Pete Dye borrowed the idea of a shared green from St. Andrews, creating a huge shared 18th green between the River Course and the Meadow Valley Course.

MILWAUKEE COUNTRY CLUB

You beat them with your game; you don't beat them with your distance.
—Manuel de la Torre, Top 100 instructor and teaching professional at MCC

Shortly after I introduced myself to Bob Milbourne, my host at Milwaukee Country Club the next day, he asked, "How did you like Black Wolf Run?" I shared my opinion, and he then revealed that prior to becoming executive director of the Greater Milwaukee Committee, he worked for Herb Kohler and was in charge of developing the two golf courses. Oops! Open mouth, insert foot. I was not off to a good start with this guy, I thought.

MCC was fantastic. When Pete Dye was asked about MCC, he thought for a few moments and then said, "Great grass." MCC is in pristine condition, featuring streams, fast greens, and challenging bunkers. On Number 11, I hit into a greenside bunker on such a steep face that I could hardly get a stance in the trap to hit the ball, but I got it on the green and two-putted for my bogey. Bob and I became friends, and a few months later, he invited me back to play in the MCC Invitational. We played in both his and my invitationals for three years, and I went with Bob to the Tournament Players Championship for three years in a row. As if he weren't busy enough, Bob was chairman of the board of the Greater Milwaukee Open Golf Tournament. The PGA tour organizers met every year at the TPC, and I went along for the ride, with clubhouse passes and all. Bob and I subsequently played a few other Top 100 courses together, and through him I met Johnny Koss (the Koss headphone Koss), who is also working on playing the Top 100, but he still has a way to go.

Aside from being a wonderful course, MCC has one of the Top 100 golf instructors in the United States, Manuel de la Torre, who teaches MCC members and has taught many PGA and LPGA players as well. And I made another discovery: Not only are golf courses and instructors rated, but so are locker rooms. You guessed it: MCC has one of the Top 50 locker rooms in the U.S., with its classic mesh lockers, beautiful wood paneling, and even a sandwich bar.

I was told there are 10 really difficult holes and eight impossible ones. I'm just trying to work out which the 10 are.

—Lee Westwood, after his practice round for the PGA Championship

Although it was 10 years later that I returned to play Whistling Straits, the third Wisconsin Top 100 course bears comparing to the other two. Although Whistling Straits is in Kohler, it is not inland like Black Wolf Run; it sits on the shore of Lake Michigan. Architect Pete Dye took a flat former military encampment and moved in 800,000 cubic yards of dirt to create a lakeside links of drifting dunes topped with colorful grasses. The bunkers are too numerous to count. If someone blindfolded you and dropped you here in the open, rugged, and windswept terrain you would have no idea that you were in Wisconsin, let alone the United States. You would be more likely to think you were in Ireland.

Whistling Straits is a walking course only. I played it with Michael Daly, one of the top-ranking amateurs in Wisconsin. The caddies were helpful even though the course had only been open a few months, and watching Michael Daly negotiate that course from the tips was a thing of beauty. I had a tough day in the trees. Next to Pebble Beach, Whistling Straits may be the best golf resort in the U.S. It came on the list almost immediately after it was built in 1998 and in 2004 hosted the PGA Championship. It is the first course to get such an award prior to being completed.

It, too, is a stern test of golf, until the wind dies down and the beast becomes somewhat tamer. The par-3 17th directly borders Lake Michigan. It is protected by wooded planks in front and a 20-foot plunge to the lakeshore on the left. The 500-yard finishing hole requires a monstrous and accurate drive just to reach the fairway, and then you must negotiate a cloverleaf green that, according to Darren Clark, "depending on the pin placement could leave players with dogleg putts." All of the holes have names: 17 and 18 are called "Pinched Nerve" and "Dyeabolical," respectively. Shaun Michael, the defending PGA Champion in 2004, said, "I had a few words of my own I wanted to call them."

If you ask Pete Dye, he'll tell you that building Whistling Straits was a "once in a lifetime thing." That's saying something for one of the world's leading golf-course architects.

a golfer's dream

new york, new york

QUAKER RIDGE

Quaker Ridge is the most underrated golf course in the New York area, because it has never been host course to a major championship. I'd like to go on record as saying it would be a tough test of golf for any tournament— the U.S. Open and the PGA included.

—Jimmy Demaret

Before I embarked on my Top 100 quest, I'd spent a lot of time in New York City and I'd never once thought of golf. But many of the Top 100 golf courses are near New York City; in fact, 18 of them lie within a 75-mile radius of the Empire State Building. In the summer of 1995, I went back to New York to play three of them: Quaker Ridge, Stanwich, and Maidstone.

Quaker Ridge, often referred to as "Tillie's Treasure" (after its golf architect), shares a fence line with its famous neighbor, Winged Foot. While at Winged Foot, I had asked several people if they knew any members at Quaker Ridge. I kept coming up with "No!" I later found out that Winged Foot is primarily Catholic and Quaker Ridge has a primarily Jewish membership. Evan Schiller, a friend I met through the Shivas Irons Society, had been a pro at Quaker Ridge, and I planned a trip to New York hoping to play the course with him. He couldn't make it, so I called my friend Steve Ral-bovsky, who was then a record executive at Arista Records. Months earlier he had said he knew a couple of members at Quaker Ridge. He called Geoff Mennin, a music attorney and member of the club, and Dave Hart, who managed Linda Eder (I'd presented her in con-cert several times), and we were off to Quaker Ridge. I wore my

"America's Guest" hat tall and proud since I knew these people would be good business connections, and Mennin, especially, was very interested in my quest. We had a great time.

As lore has it, during the Revolutionary War, George Washington slumbered near his beleaguered continental troops under a great oak as he prepared to do battle with the British troops. That oak grows to the right of Quaker Ridge's 10th hole.

Quaker Ridge is every bit as challenging a test of golf as either of the Winged Foot courses and is a far more beautiful course. However, the club largely has avoided the spotlight of hosting national tournaments. I had lunch with Goeff, Dave, and Steve, reminisced about our wonderful round at Quaker Ridge, and then left to meet Evan Schiller. I had another Top 100 course to play that afternoon in Connecticut.

STANWICH CLUB

Oh golf is for smellin' heather and walkin' fast across the countryside and feelin' the wind and watchin' the sun go down and seein' yer friends hit good shots and hittin' some yourself. It's love and it's feelin' the splendor of this good world.

—Shivas Irons, from Golf in the Kingdom

I met Evan Schiller through my connection to the Shivas Irons Society. I had read the book Golf in the Kingdom and was fascinated by it. If you haven't read it, you should. It tells the story of a golfer who plays a round at the original golf course in Scotland and has a life-changing experience with the golf pro he plays with named Shivas Irons. Shivas Irons believes that golf is a metaphor for life. The things we live out on the golf course are but a microcosm of the things we experience in life. He proceeds to discuss these lessons and how they relate to golf.

I was so taken with the book that when I learned that the Esalen Institute was hosting a five-day "Golf in the Kingdom" workshop, I signed up immediately. Esalen sits on a 100-foot-high cliff above the Pacific Ocean in Big Sur, California. There were 12 participants in the workshop from all over the United States. We played golf, did a few golf drills, but mostly we talked about life using golf as a metaphor. Let me give you an example of one exercise: We divided into three foursomes and headed out to the lawn of Esalen. Our instructions were to choose a captain, play three holes, and have fun. Each hole was designated by a four-foot circle drawn on the lawn, and when you were inside that circle, you were deemed to have holed out.

At the conclusion of the round, we were asked several questions: How did you pick the captain? Did someone volunteer, or did you suggest someone? Did you vote? How was the selection made? What role did you play in that selection and why? Did you count your strokes? Did you view it as a competition? If so, why or why not? Did you watch the other teams to see how you were doing in relation to them? If so, why or why not? Did you hit first, second, third, or fourth on the first hole? Why did you pick that position? Did you support your fellow team members or put them down if they hit a bad shot? How about yourself? Were you there to have fun or to compete or both? Take a few minutes and think about some of these questions and your answers. You might learn something about yourself. We had a discussion that lasted more than an hour following that 25-minute exercise.

The golf pro at this workshop was Fred Schoemaker, author of Extraordinary Golf. He was very impressive, and I went on to take two golf clinics from him. I became friends with a couple of the instructors, one of whom was Evan Schiller.

After my lunch at Quaker Ridge, I met up with Evan Schiller and we were off to the Stanwich Club for a one o'clock tee time. The Stanwich Golf Club is in Greenwich, Connecticut (about 20 miles from Quaker Ridge). Two courses, two different states, one day: It felt like a landmark. Evan and I met Andy Nusbaum, a VP at Golf Digest, who we both knew from the Shivas Irons Society and who was hosting us that afternoon.

Stanwich Club was founded in 1964 and designed by William and David Gordon, names I had never heard of before or since.

Long, tight, and relatively flat, with trees lining all 18 fairways, Stanwich is truly an imposing test of golf. Perhaps its most memorable features are the Gordon-style greens, some say the fastest in the metropolitan area, canted severely from back to front and bunkered tenaciously at their front corners, with lakes and streams that come into play on eight holes. Andy is a former golf pro, and playing with Evan and Andy that day was quite the treat. They both tore up the course.

One of the things we talk about in the Shivas Irons Society is finding more of the fun in the game and less of the stress. On Number 12, Andy hit a shot that hooked slightly into the greenside woods. It was going to take quite a recovery to get it near the pin. Andy was visibly upset. All it took from me was a "look" and a drawled out, "Now Andy," and he made a complete attitude change. "Thanks, Larry," he said, "This is an opportunity shot. I can't hit a thrilling recovery shot unless I hit it in an undesirable place first." He hit a low punch through some tree trunks that I couldn't believe, landing 10 feet from the flag. We all watched in amazement. He sunk the putt for par.

After my in-depth exposure to Golf in the Kingdom, I decided that as part of being "America's Guest," I would give everyone a copy of Golf in the Kingdom. So I contacted the publisher and ordered 40 copies. (I got them wholesale.) At each course I played, I explained a little bit about the book and what it had meant to me, and at the end of the round, I gave a copy to my host with a thank-you note written on the inside cover.

MAIDSTONE

Easily the best laid out links I have ever played anywhere. There, in order to negotiate the round properly, you must be a master in the art of both scientific slicing and pulling, and be able to get the full measure of every conceivable stroke that occurs in the game, or else you can be subject to some penalty—in short, every shot has to be played for all it's worth. That is GOLF!

—Walter Travis, Golf Illustrated

The next day Evan and I were up at the crack of dawn, driving to the farthest end of Long Island to play Maidstone. At 4:30 a.m., in the truck traffic on the Cross Island Expressway, I found myself holding the steering wheel tighter and tighter. I was so stressed out when we finally got through it that I felt ready for bed. It took three hours of driving to get to the farthest reaches of Long Island and, finally, the calm of East Hampton.

In addition to being a golf pro, Evan is a professional golf-course photographer, and Maidstone was going to hire him to photograph its golf course. For me, it was a fantasy trip; for Evan, who had never been there before, it was a reconnaissance trip to prepare to photograph the course at a later date. So we spent the day playing golf, enjoying the nearly abandoned surroundings and looking at the course through the eyes of a photographer.

Maidstone was created in its current form in the 1920s by Willie Park. It lies in East Hampton and, to some people's thinking, may be the most exclusive club on Long Island. The south end of this peninsula is framed by a thousand-yard stretch of sand dunes with the Atlantic Ocean just over the other side. The soil is sandy throughout; it truly looks and plays like the links courses in Scotland: windy, windy, windy, with sun-baked, non-irrigated fairways and plenty of dunes in which to lose your ball. It's one of the most understated clubs that I have played, giving the impression that, "no one has any money here," but only the very elite can get in. Go figure.

Some detractors of the course point to the fact that it is only 6,400 yards, but when the wind is blowing, they are 6,400 challenging yards. The dunes, ocean, and ponds will make fantastic photos on Evan's return. If it hadn't been for Evan, I might never have played here. When I was at the National Golf Links of America, I met a Maidstone member in the locker room, who had given me his card and said to call about playing Maidstone, but all my calls went unreturned. That is as close as I have come to meeting anyone associated with the course. I shot 89 and Evan shot a smooth 73—one over. We watched the sunset over Long Island Sound and went to dinner.

a golfer's dream

sweet home chicago

CHICAGO GOLF CLUB

There are remarkable people, and then there are geniuses. Often, those geniuses have personality traits that seem extreme in one way or another. They may become so deeply involved in one activity it becomes an obsession. Charles Blair Macdonald was one of those extraordinary people who saw something he liked, and promptly turned it into a lifetime quest, then he led his nation into the same love affair. Golf was his love.

—Bob Weisgerber

When my cousin Hank Wilmer was a VP at a bank in Chicago, one of his coworkers, Jim Hasten, was a member at Chicago Golf Club. Hank got us both an invitation to play Chicago Golf Club, located in Wheaton, Illinois, about half an hour from O'Hare Airport. I think Hank was as excited to get an invitation as I was. I was scheduled to arrive at 9 a.m. and fly home that evening. That was a new one for me: Fly in for a round of golf and fly out in time to be home for dinner. Hank picked me up at O'Hare at 10:15, and the weather was sunny, brisk, and very windy. So windy, in fact, that when he popped the trunk to put my bags in, the wind caught the lid and sprung the latch. We spent the next 30 minutes trying to get the trunk closed. Windy City indeed!

We drove to Wheaton, a small suburb northwest of Chicago, and as we were looking for the entrance drive, we finally saw what may be the smallest sign ever made for a golf course. I don't want to give you the impression that this place enjoys its privacy, but if the sign were any smaller you would need a microscope to read it.

We pulled up to the bag drop and the man who took our clubs asked if we were "guests of Jim." As we parked the car in the nearly empty lot, I asked Hank, "Do you think that they have that high a level of awareness of members and their guests? Or are we just the only ones here?" We walked into the modest clubhouse, and it was clearly the latter. It was almost noon on a Sunday, and we were the only people in the locker room and the only people at lunch (to my delight, peanut butter and jelly was at the top of the menu). Our threesome was one of only four groups that played the course all day. Why? CGC has only 106 members. There may be clubs with smaller memberships, but not on the Top 100.

Jim Hasten, our host, got into CGC because his wife's uncle was president of the club and Jim had played there with him for years. Not exactly direct blood lineage, but close enough. On October 1, 1993, he and Jim were playing one of their many rounds together when on the back nine he had a heart attack and died on the course in Jim's arms.

Chicago Golf Club claims to be the oldest 18-hole golf course in the United States, and it probably is, although there are people who will dispute that claim. It was built in 1894 by C.B. Macdonald and is one of the five founding clubs of the United States Golf Association, along with St. Andrews in Hastings, New York; Newport (Rhode Island) Country Club; the Country Club in Boston; and Shinnecock Hills in New York.

CGC has hosted three U.S. Opens, but that was many years ago. The course has one set of men's tees at 6,574 yards par 70, so its length prevents it from hosting any major tournaments these days. There are no plantings either: What you play is what you get. There is minimal service in the clubhouse, and the snack shack at the turn is self-serve on the honor system: Take what you want and write it down.

The summer of 1995 was unseasonably hot and humid, and the weather took its toll on CGC. The course lost many of its fairways and some of its greens, which were just growing back. The day started with a 450-yard par 4 into a screaming wind, and it was a challenge from there. On much of the course, we played on dead grass, nearly on dirt. I shot 89 that day and was damn proud of it. I didn't get to see CGC anywhere near its best. This is one course I would love to play when it's in optimal condition, but I doubt I will ever get another invitation to play. After a quick snack, it was back to O'Hare for my 8 p.m. flight home. What a day!

a golfer's dream

jersey boys

PINE VALLEY

To be able to play the most challenging golf courses in the world is as good as it gets. That is a dream vacation.

—*Terry McAuliffe, former Democratic National Committee chairman*

Terry McAuliffe is quoted in a New York Times article on the Jack Abramoff scandal, which closely intertwines golf and congressional lobbying. The great golf courses are an aphrodisiac to even the world's most powerful politicians and businessmen. Pine Valley is consistently rated the best of the best.

Nearly every golfer who has picked up a club wants to play Augusta National. Any golfer who can afford it plays Pebble Beach. But in almost every ranking, worldwide or national, Pine Valley is always on top, No. 1, primo, the Mecca, numero uno. Its memberships (and guest rounds) are highly sought. Although not as exclusive as Augusta, which has a couple of hundred members, Pine Valley has nearly 1,000 members from the elite of society across the world. My cousin Andy Kneeter's business associate Gene Gardner is a member, and he agreed to host Andy, Barclay Douglas, and me at Pine Valley.

On October 10, 1996, Andy and I spent the night at Barclay's house, and the next morning we set off for Pine Valley, across the Delaware River approximately 30 miles north of Philadelphia in New Jersey. As we pulled up to the guard shack, I saw the smallest Police Dept. and Fire Dept. signs that I have ever laid eyes on. I assume the golf course has been incorporated as a township, so it must govern itself—in more ways than one, I can assure you. I wonder if the golf school is K-12.

In 1912, George Crump acquired 184 acres of scrub-pine land to create Pine Valley and brought in all the great golf-course architects of the day to see the property and contribute any ideas they may have had about routing a course there. Harry Colt was hired as a consultant, but the vast majority of the design work was that of George Crump himself. He lived on the property and oversaw the construction of all but the final three holes, which were being completed when he died. He never saw the whole thing. He had never designed another golf course, but no one tops him in the golf-course architect rankings.

The expanse of sandy scrub pines was so unappealing that skeptics wondered if Crump could even grow grass on it. To create Pine Valley, he directed the removal of more than 22,000 stumps that had to be pulled out with special steam winches and horse-drawn cables because dynamite only blew up the sand around the stump. Marshlands were drained, dams built, and underbrush cleared away. Many called it "Crump's Folly," but his vision turned out to be genius.

I was ready for a difficult day of golf. Everyone said I would never break 100 on my first visit here. But I parred Number 1 and ended the day with a 92. This is one hard course, par 70 with a rating of 74 and a slope of 153, and it's only 6,667 yards. I didn't think the USGA gave out slope ratings that high.

On Number 2, Barclay, who was a 4- or 5-handicap at the time, hit a perfect drive down the middle of this 375-yard hole. Then he hit what appeared to be a perfect 6-iron, but it barely rolled over the back edge of the green. The green is severely sloped from back to front and the pin was all the way in the front. After a very delicate chip onto the green, he was surprised to hear his caddie say, "Bye-bye," as it slid off the front into one of the famous waste bunkers of Pine Valley, where he stayed for eight shots. Two putts later, Barclay was writing down 12 for the hole. Number 7 is home to what may be the most famous hazard in golf, "Hell's Half Acre," a waste bunker that stretches from the 285-yard mark to the 380-

yard mark on this par 5. The 10th hole seems to be a benign 145-yard par 3, but it has what appears to be a tiny bunker in the front left called "The Devil's Asshole." Lots of balls seem to find it, and many golfers get very exasperated in there. Enough said!

Number 15 is a 590-yard par 5 uphill into the wind. Whew! I hit driver, 3-wood, 3-wood, and 6-iron, and two putted for a 6. They were all pretty good shots, too. It was exhausting. One famous Pine Valley story is about a golfer who had made a substantial bet that he could play the course without losing more than 10 golf balls. He was seen putting his ball across the bridge over the stream on 16, in order to win his bet and keep his ball for three more holes. The caddies at Pine Valley are invaluable, and they have eyes like hawks. The good news is a caddie can find almost any ball that finds its way into the scrub. The bad news is, he stands there and expects you to hit it. Bastard!

Tons of other great stories surround this great club. Jack Nicklaus played Pine Valley on his honeymoon. He and Barbara were driving by the course and Jack said, "Here's Pine Valley. Let's stop and have a look." Nicklaus, who recently had won the U.S. Amateur, was immediately recognized by a member in the pro shop who invited him to play. Since there are no women allowed, someone courteously accompanied Barbara around the perimeter of the course so she could catch a glimpse of Jack on a few holes. Only Jack Nicklaus could get away with something like that on his honeymoon. Then there's the story of a man who hit three birdies and a par on the opening holes. At the 4th green, which returns to the front door of the clubhouse, he retired to the bar. "It can only go downhill from here," he said as he retired his sticks for the day. Pine Valley is a men-only club, although women are allowed to play on Sunday afternoons. Bob Hope once said, "My favorite stop on tour is Valley Forge Music Center because I get to play golf at Pine Valley."

Several years ago, the club hired Tom Fazio to build a "second-shot course" that replicates the approach shots of all 18 holes. Unfortunately, I didn't get to play the short course. Recently, two members were suspended for selling guest rounds for $10,000 each. Pine Valley hosts only one tournament, the annual Crump Cup, which allows public viewing and is played in late September. It's the easiest way to see the course.

immaculate reception

AUGUSTA NATIONAL

Watching the Masters on TV is like attending a church service. Announcers speak in hushed pious tones as if to convince us that something of great meaning and historical importance is taking place. What we are actually seeing is grown men hitting little balls with sticks.

—*Tom Gilmore, San Francisco Chronicle*

I just dropped a three-foot putt for par on Number 12 at Augusta National, my first par of the day. I am at the apex of Amen Corner, a place I never dreamt I would be standing. Jack Nicklaus calls this "the hardest hole in all of tournament golf." Gary Player calls this 155-yard hole "the hardest par 3 in the world." The 12th green at Augusta was the first temperature-controlled green in the world; water pipes were installed underneath the green to keep its surface temperature at a constant 70 degrees Fahrenheit.

The 12th hole at Augusta National may be the most recognizable hole in golf because it is viewed on TV by millions of golf fans every year during the spring ritual that is the Masters Tournament. Every golfer dreams of playing this hole. But not many do. The day I played Augusta National was one of the club's busiest, with six foursomes on the grounds. I know because there is a board in the clubhouse that lists "members on premises."

If playing golf at Augusta National is the most coveted four hours of every golfer in America, how did I get on? I got lucky when I met a member of Augusta early in the third year of my quest. My office was on the 18th floor of the Foshay Tower in downtown Minneapolis. The Foshay Tower, a 27-story tribute to the Washington Monument, was the tallest building west of the Mississippi when it was built in 1929. There was one restroom on every floor: men's on even floors and women's on the odd floors. The men whose offices were on odd floors could choose to go up or down to the men's room. Wheelock Whitney, whose office was on 19, chose to come down. I knew him as a community leader who once had run for governor of Minnesota and for the U.S. Senate. I also knew he was one of four or five Minnesota residents who are members of Augusta National. I greeted him regularly in the restroom. We made small talk from time to time, and then one day I swallowed hard and tried to muster up my courage. When it would not muster, I blurted out the question I had been dying to ask: "You're a member at Augusta National, right?"

"Yes," he replied casually, but he had to know what was coming next. When I told him about my quest, he seemed interested, and then I hit the follow-up: "What am I going to have to do to play there?" (It seemed to be a more diplomatic approach than coming right out and asking him to invite me.) "Become very good friends with a member," he said as we both walked out the door and headed back to our respective offices.

So I began a two-year initiative to become Wheelock's friend. I found out his birthday and invited him to lunch. At lunch, we discovered that we had many friends and interests in common. Amazingly, he had helped my best friend get a scholarship to Dartmouth. I invited him to play golf at my club. Wheelock was an owner of the Minnesota Vikings at the time. So late that summer when the Vikings were scheduled to play the team's charity golf tournament, I called him to ask if he would like to play as my guest in a foursome, as if I didn't already know that he would be playing. He very kindly said that he had reserved a foursome and would I like join his?

Throughout the round, he boasted about me, his new friend, who was playing the Top 100. We played with another friend of his and Randall McDaniel, an offensive lineman for the Vikings. Randall is a gentle giant, whose shoulders are almost as wide as he is tall, and a truly nice guy. He could hit the ball well over 300 yards with a 5 wood; his direction, however, was questionable.

We had to use three tee shots from everyone (we were actually a five-some), and when it came to the 17th hole we still needed to use one of Randall's tee shots and one of mine. Like every earlier tee shot, Randall hit it far. But this one was also down the middle of our fairway. I was also in the middle, about a hundred yards behind him, which meant that on the 18th hole only my tee shot would be usable. Eighteen was a 180-yard par 3 over wetlands. In my typical no-holds-barred style, I said, "Okay, Wheelock, since the whole team is riding on my tee shot, what would I have to do to get a trip to Augusta out of this?" I thought sure the answer would be a hole-in-one, but he said, "Get it on the green." Although I had tripled the pressure on myself, I hit a high, drifting draw right at the green and silently cheered as I felt certain I had accomplished my task. But as we approached the green, I saw that my ball had rolled a mere few inches onto the fringe, to which Wheelock said, "Close! I guess I can take you to play golf in Atlanta." We all had a good laugh, but I died a little inside. However, my day at Augusta was not far off.

The following spring, two buddies and I had been hiking and biking in the Canyon Lands and Arches National Park in Utah. When I got to the Salt Lake airport to fly home, I called my office to check my voicemail. "You have one message," the voicemail lady chirped. I pressed one and heard, "This is your friend Wheelock Whitney. I am down in Augusta with my brother and his wife. My daughter was going to join us, but she canceled. If you can be here tomorrow night for dinner, we can play Augusta National together the following day. If you can make it, call my secretary and give her the details of your trip." I couldn't believe my ears, so I played it again with my friends David and Ronnie huddled at the earpiece with me. I heard it again, they confirmed it, and I was ready to high-five the whole airport. When I arrived in Minneapolis around 6 p.m., I had to plan a trip, clear my schedule, and leave the next morning. It would be a late night.

I burst into the house, dying to tell my wife what had happened.

Then I hit the phone. First I had to find Augusta on the map. I was not even sure how far it was from Atlanta. I found a flight to Atlanta and thought I would rent a car and drive to Augusta. Every car-rental company that I called in Atlanta was sold out. Damn, what do I do now? I found a flight from Atlanta to Augusta on Delta Airlines. I got my tickets and called Wheelock's secretary—by this time it was well after midnight—voicemail is a good thing. I honestly don't know how many messages she got from me the next morning, but she had my itinerary.

The next morning I was up at the crack of dawn, my heart pounding excitedly! I drove to the airport and flew to Atlanta. During my two-hour layover in Atlanta, I suddenly realized I had no idea where the club was, where I would be staying, or how I would get there from the airport. So I called Augusta National (thankfully the club has a listed phone number). "Good afternoon, Augusta National Golf Club," said the friendly voice on the other end. "Hello, I'm looking for Wheelock Whitney. I am a guest of his, and I'm on my way there." (I felt an overwhelming need to explain myself to the receptionist.) "Is this Mr. Berle?" My name was even properly pronounced; I was stunned. "Yes." "Mr. Whitney is not available, but you are arriving on Delta Airlines at 5 p.m., from Atlanta, correct?" "Yes," I mumbled, still stunned. "We will have a car to meet you and bring you to the club." "Thank you," I said nonchalantly, but when I hung up, I screeched, "Yes-sssss!!!!!!" I couldn't believe it. Everything was going my way, and somehow I was upgraded to first class on my short 45-minute flight to Augusta. To say that I felt like the king of the world would be an understatement. A car and driver would be waiting to take me to golf's Holy Grail.

There is an old joke about a man who goes into a confessional. "Father, I am 80 years old and last night I had sex with a beautiful 20-year-old girl." The voice on the other side of the confessional says, "Is that a Jewish accent I hear?" "Yes, Father," he responds. "Well, why are you telling this to me?" "I'm telling everybody," the old Jewish man responds proudly. That is just how I felt. I wanted to walk the aisle of the plane and tell everyone that I was going to play Augusta National. But I contained myself. I did, however, tell the guy sitting next to me, and he was duly impressed.

As I deplaned I saw the driver with the sign: "Mr. Berle." He was easy to find as the Augusta airport is quite small and has only one baggage carousel. The driver was a friendly guy who wouldn't let me lift a finger with my bags. The setting sun cast a golden hue over Augusta, Georgia, and I felt like I was in another world. My driver was a jazz musician on the side, so we talked music for the entire trip. He even knew James Brown, who lived in Augusta and whom I had presented in concert in Minneapolis a few years earlier.

Suddenly I was transported from my world of music to my golf world. As the sun dropped below the horizon, we turned left onto Magnolia Lane, the famed entrance to Augusta National. I paid full attention, taking in every bush, tree, blade of grass, and finally the guard shack. The guard casually waved us through; we passed the clubhouse on the right (possibly the most recognizable clubhouse in the world) and pulled into the driveway of the four cabins nestled between the clubhouse and Augusta's famous par-3 course. Standing just outside the front door of the Firestone Cabin were Wheelock and his brother Kim and Kim's wife, Helen. I was trembling with excitement, and my excitement rubbed off on them. (A quick word here about the battle between the National Organization of Women and Augusta National. Augusta may not allow women as members, but they are friendly to women in every other way. There is no restriction on their being guests or what they may do as guests. Helen was treated with the same respect by the club as both Kim and I were.) My eyes couldn't possibly drink enough in! I was ready to tee it up right then, even though it was nearly dark. Bags to my room and we were off to dinner in the clubhouse. Luckily, I had a coat and tie with me, and I needed a coat and tie to eat in the dining room. Wheelock wore his member's green jacket. Members are required to wear their green jackets in the dining room.

Here I was dining at Augusta National. Pinch me, or maybe hit me over the head with a two-by-four. Never in a million years did I envision myself here, sitting in the dining room where America's power brokers dine. Maybe I was sitting in a chair that former President Eisenhower sat in! I shared with my dinner partners the feeling that overcame me as our car had turned onto Magnolia Drive to enter Augusta National. Wheelock looked me in the eye and replied, "I've been coming here for years, Larry, and my heart still skips a beat whenever I turn onto Magnolia Drive." The menu was limited, but the waiter informed me that I could order anything I want, whether it's on the menu or not. As I pondered my choices, one was made for me. "Larry, you're in the South, so have some collard greens," Wheelock suggested. I couldn't imagine anything worse, but I ordered them and ate them. That's what good guests do. If there's one thing this quest has taught me, it's how to be a good guest.

After dinner Wheelock took me on a tour. First stop, the crow's nest. This is the small cupola of the clubhouse where the amateurs who are competing in the Masters stay. I am sure I could go through the list of amateurs who have played the Masters and find that many greats slept in these meager quarters. "I want to sleep here," I thought. We walked down a flight of stairs to the Masters Champions Locker Room. This locker room is used one week each year, Masters Week; the other 51 weeks a year it sits empty but for the likes of people like me who come to experience its historic aura and gaze upon the lockers of the greats: Bobby Jones, Sam Snead, Byron Nelson, Gene Sarazen, Arnold Palmer, and Jack Nicklaus. They've put on their golf shoes in here one at a time, just like me. I also imagine they've sat here after their rounds thinking about the same things I think about after a round: "What if that putt on 15 had dropped? Why didn't I play it more conservative on 13? What could my score have been?" The difference is I may just have played a $2 Nassau; they're playing for a living on the world's stage.

We visited the Masters media center, the largest permanent sports-media facility in the world. (Permanent was the key word here; the media tents for the Super Bowl and World Series are much larger, but not permanent.) Looking over the big TV screens, large leader boards, interview areas, and amphitheater-style seating for about 500 writers with chairs, desks, phones, and computer outlets, I could feel the presence of golf's great writers in search of a unique story, sweating out their deadlines.

As we let ourselves into the Butler Cabin, I imagined Jim Nance and Hootie Johnson sitting in the chairs, interviewing this year's Masters winner as last year's champion slipped the green jacket onto the new champion's shoulders. I had seen this ceremony on television so often that it felt like I was walking into a neighbor's living room that I had visited many times before.

It was late, but we weren't done. Wheelock had a guard unlock the Eisenhower cabin, which is where we spent the most time on our tour. Its walls were like a small museum of Eisenhower campaign and presidential memorabilia: "I Like Ike" pins; framed letters to and from world leaders; two wonderful paintings that Eisenhower had painted himself, one of the 12th green of Augusta. I had no idea he was a painter, and a pretty good one at that. We walked to the basement to find the biggest difference between this and the other cabins: several small bedrooms that were built to be sleeping quarters for the secret service. Back upstairs I pondered a framed series of four photos with a caption that read: "Houses I have lived in." There was a picture of a small house that Eisenhower grew up in, the barracks he lived in at Fort Benning, Georgia, while in the Army, the White House, and the cabin we were standing in. "Only in America," I thought to myself.

The Eisenhower cabin locked behind us, we strolled under the star-filled southern sky back to the Firestone Cabin. Before I retired, Wheelock said, "In case you can't sleep, call the front desk and they will put on a video of any Masters you want to watch on the TV in your room."

I think I got some sleep, but to be honest, I'm not sure. I know I had plenty of energy when I woke up. We ate breakfast and then we met our caddies and headed to the driving range. Now I knew I was practicing where the world's greatest golfers have practiced, but I soon realized that that fact wasn't making my golf swing any better. In fact, thinking about it may have been making it worse. Then it was off to the practice green. Whoa! I had expected lightning quick, I had expected major undulations, and my first practice putt confirmed those expectations in a grandiose way. Welcome to Augusta National.

We walked over to the par-3 course and teed it up. "As long as you are here you should experience it all," Wheelock said. This is probably the most famous par-3 course in the world. So famous, in fact, that a few years later someone paid $20,000 at a charity auction in Minneapolis to caddie for Tom Lehman at the Masters par-3 tournament. No one offered even a nickel to caddie for me today.

After these beautiful nine par 3s, we headed to the main course. As I stood on the first tee, I thought about the honorary starters I had watched tee off here on TV: Sam Sneed, Gene Sarazen, and Byron Nelson. I looked up the fairway and hit my first drive down the middle. I bogeyed Number 1. I was not in the middle on Number 2, and I was suddenly reminded that Augusta National has no rough (in the last few years rough has been added). All drives look pretty good until you realize that in order to be in the right spot on the green you must be in the right spot on the fairway. Believe me, you don't want to be in the wrong spot on Augusta's greens or you're going to be doing lots of putting, and I did plenty of putting, nine three-putt greens—much higher than my normal day. As we played, I realized that I had expected to recognize every hole and every fairway, but I'd forgotten that the front nine of the Masters wasn't televised until recently. Yet almost every hole is significant or historic in the world of tournament golf. During the 1954 Masters, amateur Billy Joe Patton got a hole-in-one on Number 6, a 180-yard par 3, which launched him into the lead on the last day. He didn't win, but I think he is the only amateur to ever hold a lead at the Masters. As we left the 9th green, we were met by a photographer who took a picture of our foursome and caddies. A few weeks later that picture showed up in my mailbox, and there I was grinning ear to ear.

We soon made the turn to Number 10, and I guarantee you that

I recognized everything on the back nine. When you're watching the Masters on TV, you don't see the elevation changes. I had no idea how far downhill Number 10 tumbles, much more steeply on the left side of the fairway than the right. It's enough to make a 30 to 40-yard difference in your tee shot. The ideal tee shot draws to the left side of the fairway and catches the big downhill roll, making it longer than the par 5, 13th hole.

Amen Corner was quite a welcome site for me: Hit the ball take a picture, take a picture hit the ball. Amen Corner got its name from journalist Herbert Warren Wind in 1957, when he wrote, "If you get through Amen Corner in even par, you feel a bit closer to God." Number 13, the end of Amen Corner, is as exciting to play as it appears on TV. It's a 465-yard par 5 that crosses Ray's Creek twice. The first time you cross it easily with your tee shot. Ray's Creek runs menacingly along the left side of the fairway until it gets to the green where it cuts directly across the fairway in front of the green. The creek is only a few feet wide, but it's a treacherous few feet with closely mown banks that gobble up many a disappointed golfer's ball. For us mere mortals, it tends to gobble up third shots. In the Masters, it tends to gobble up second shots. Then there are the lucky ones, like Fred Couples, who spun his second shot back off the green and it hung mysteriously on the steep bank of Ray's Creek. The perfect drive is a long, sweeping draw around the corner of the dogleg left, but I hit mine up the right side and short. The second shot was right, leaving me an 8-iron to the green. I bogeyed that one, too.

The 15th is a par 5 of 500-yards. It's the hole where Gene Sarazen hit his famous "shot heard round the world." The shallow green is fronted by a pond, and there is more water behind the green. During the fourth round of the 1935 Masters, Sarazen put his second shot in the hole from the fairway for a double-eagle 2, which brought him into a tie for the lead. He won the playoff the next day.

Number 16, the par 3 over water, turned disastrous for all of us: four tee shots, four balls in the water. Please note that we were all trying to get it over the water, unlike in Masters practice rounds where almost every pro hits his real tee shot and then tries to skip it across the pond onto the green. And those who even consider not trying are ceaselessly heckled by the crowd until they do. My second tee shot was on the right front of the green with the pin on the front left. I barely touched that putt and it wound around like a horseshoe, slowly inching its way toward the hole. I 2-putted for a 5.

I walked away wondering, "Is there any place here at Augusta National where you could putt your ball in a complete circle?"

The course was immaculate. The caddies carried bags of divot mix. My follow-through was barely completed, and I could hear the splat of divot mix filling my divot from the caddie's bag. "This stuff is so potent you could grow grass on the hood of your car," he said. There are lots of famous stories about the caddies of Augusta National, but one I especially like is about a caddie taking his golfer between nines to the practice sand trap to show him how to get out. Seems the caddies had a bet on the game, and he wanted his man to win.

Augusta National came to life on its 365 acres in January 1933. It was the vision of the greatest golfer of his day, Bobby Jones. He enlisted Cliff Robertson to help raise the money to buy the land and the great Alister MacKenzie to design the course. MacKenzie completed his design but never lived to see it in its completed form. Everyone who plays the course will attest to the fact that it is an architectural masterpiece, with merely 50 bunkers on the entire course. The design offers plenty of challenge, making excessive bunkering unnecessary. Membership is made of the political and business power brokers of America. A close look at the rosters shows that almost all of them are retired and the average age looks to be well over 70. Bill Gates may be the youngest at age 47, but not the richest; his buddy Warren Buffet is a member, too.

The elevation change on Number 18 is another spot TV viewers cannot fully appreciate. I hit a solid tee shot through the famous chute of trees to the middle of the fairway. But I had a long way to go to the green and at least two clubs of uphill. I wasn't thinking about hitting it past the pin and spinning it back to the hole as Jim Nance has described on TV so many times, I just wanted to get it there. But I came up 20 yards short, pitched it on to one of the world's most televised greens and 2-putted for my bogey.

Suddenly my dream day came to a close as we strolled away from the 18th green, where I had watched the thrill of victory and the agony of defeat so many times on the final Sundays of the Masters. I spent $250 on logo merchandise in the pro shop, and I'm guessing that amount was lower than what many guests typically spend. A quick shower and change and my driver pulled up to whisk me back to the airport. As I threw my clubs in the trunk, Wheelock lowered his voice and said, "One last thing, Larry, when you wake up tomorrow, remember this really happened. It was not a dream."

a golfer's dream

nothing could be finer

PINEHURST NO. 2

This is the finest test of championship golf.

—*Donald Ross, course architect*

The weekend before Thanksgiving, Annie and I took a trip to Pinehurst. We met my friend Gary Albrecht and played two courses on the Top 100, Pinehurst Number 2 and Country Club of North Carolina. We stayed at the Inn, a fantastic hotel. Pinehurst is the home of the North-South Amateur each year, and the Inn's halls are filled with photos and memorabilia of the early days of some of the greatest golfers on the PGA tour.

The first day we played at Country Club of North Carolina, which is breathtaking. It's a private club that was designed by Ellis Maples, who I now have the utmost respect for as a golf architect. He designed a couple of other courses at Pinehurst resort as well. Country Club of North Carolina is cut through the pines with lots of elevation changes, and I would love to play here again.

The next day we played the legendary Pinehurst No. 2. This course is on everyone's Top 10, but to be honest I don't know why. I liked it, but I didn't love it. Donald Ross, who designed the course, was born in 1872 in Dornoch, Scotland. He came to the United States in 1899 without a penny to his name at the invitation of a Harvard professor who helped him get a job as head pro at Oakley Country Club. He was a fiercely competitive golfer who won three North-South Opens and a fifth place in the 1903 U.S. Open. In 1900, he took the job as head pro at Pinehurst, where he began designing golf courses.

Ross is probably the most prolific designer who ever lived; he designed more than 400 golf courses, a third or a quarter of which he never stepped foot on. At the peak of his career, he employed approximately 3,000 people. Eleven of his courses are on the Golf Digest Top 100. Eighteen U.S. Opens have been played on Donald Ross courses. Although he was bitter after losing the bid to design Augusta National, he then devoted himself to making Pinehurst No. 2 the greatest golf course in the nation. He lived at Pinehurst for many years, and he was constantly tinkering with the design of No. 2. Most people say it is his best design. I have played several of his other courses (Oakland Hills and Salem Country Club) that I liked much more, but I am clearly in the minority.

The price to play Pinehurst had not yet skyrocketed, so Annie and I played it two days in a row. The rough was dormant in the fall so it was not particularly scenic. No. 2 is not only challenging from tee to green, but almost every green is crowned, so even a well hit shot onto the green may roll off into a collection area, and there are many of those, which can become frustrating. If you're a good chipper and putter, then you can score well on this course, because you'll be doing a lot of chipping. If not—well, have a nice day.

california here i come

VALLEY CLUB OF MONTECITO

Annie and I spent the month of January 1996 in Carmel in a rented house. One day we drove down to Santa Barbara to play the Valley Club with Lawrence Gamble and his brother Tom. I'd met Lawrence at the "Golf in the Kingdom" workshop and we'd kept in touch (in fact, I kept in touch with several people in that workshop and still keep in touch with a couple of them). Lawrence was as excited to play the Valley Club as I was; I guess his brother Tom rarely invites him to play there.

It seldom rains in Santa Barbara; in fact, it hadn't rained in two months, but it rained that day, almost all day. It began raining on the second hole and never let up. After Number 5, Annie quit and went in; Tom, Lawrence, and I trudged on. At the turn, Tom said, "When I get back to the office, no one will believe me when I tell them where I have been." It seems there are so few bad weather days in Santa Barbara that no one in his right mind keeps playing golf in the rain. On the 15th hole, Tom's club flew from his soaking wet hand as a duck hook flew off the tee. "That's it for me—you guys can finish without me." Lawrence and I moved like drowned rats to the 16th hole and turned it into an adventure to make it to the finish. It was wet, it was sloppy, the holes were all full of water, and standing water was beginning to accumulate on the greens— but we were gonna get it done and we did.

The Valley Club was designed by Alister MacKenzie in 1929. He designed Augusta National and Cypress Point and is perhaps the greatest golf architect in history. This place is a gem with immaculate greens and truly beautifully designed holes. Even in all that slop and muck, I shot 88. I would love to play this gem on a beautiful day.

florida keys

JUPITER HILLS

Ninety percent of this game is half mental.

—*Yogi Berra*

Bob Milbourne, who I met playing Milwaukee Country Club, was very helpful in my quest to play the Top 100. I met Johnny Koss through him, and Johnny was on a mission to play the Top 100 as well. He had all the courses that had ever appeared on both the Golf Digest and Golf Magazine lists in a database that he kept on his computer. Wherever his business travels took him, he played one of these courses. Later in my quest, Johnny and his dad helped me quite a bit as well.

George Kaiser, a friend of Bob's, is a member at Jupiter Hills in Florida. Bob called George and arranged for me to play Jupiter Hills. When George said I could bring a friend, I called Howard Wechsler, who lives in Miami.

Howard and I met at the "Golf in the Kingdom" workshop at Esalen and hit it off immediately. He runs a small company in Miami that sells steel shelving. Howard is a former professional jai-alai player, one of few Americans and perhaps the only Jewish American who ever played jai-alai professionally.

A few days before the game, I checked in with George, who said, "I have a fourth and it's Nicklaus." I couldn't believe my ears, although I knew Nicklaus lived in the area. Howard and I showed up nervous and excited, and George introduced us to "Ab Nicklaus" (short for Abner), who owned a financial services company in Milwaukee. It wasn't until we reached the turn that I told them who I had been expecting and we all had a good laugh on me.

No. 84 in the rankings, Jupiter Hills is located several miles inland in Tequesta, Florida. George Fazio (Tom Fazio's uncle) designed the course in 1970, with Tom's help. Although it's called Jupiter Hills and the clubhouse sits on the highest point in the county, most of us who don't live in Florida wouldn't call it hilly.

It was windy, however, two to three clubs of wind all day, but otherwise pretty nondescript. It's certainly a good course, but not one that I would hurry back to play again. I shot in the low 90s (the wind was really a challenge), and Howard carded an 87.

Golf is very much like gambling. Hitting the jackpot on a one-armed bandit is like hitting that one good shot. You're not going to walk away. You're convinced it will happen again.

—*George Peper, golf writer*

SEMINOLE GOLF CLUB

I have been looking forward to this day: Seminole is a storied and exclusive club; and my friend Kim Whitney (brother to Wheelock, my host at Augusta), who lives in Minneapolis, is hosting Howard and me. Seminole was designed in 1929 by Donald Ross and sits right on the ocean in North Palm Beach, Florida. It is ranked No. 11 and deserves it. I've played many Donald Ross courses now, and some are outstanding (Seminole, Oakland Hills, Salem Country Club, for example) and others are just so-so. Ross was a very prolific designer with 413 golf courses to his credit. So many, in fact, that it is doubtful that he actually had time to visit and design all the courses he is credited with in his lifetime. Ross, who died in 1948, probably designed one-third of his courses from photos or topographical maps and never actually saw the land or visited the sites. Another one-third he visited only once or twice. Therefore, there is a great variation in the quality of Donald Ross courses across the United States. I am sure Seminole is one where he spent some time. As well known and respected as he is today as a golf-course designer, Ross didn't take in the kind of fees golf architects do today, and he died with no money.

Howard and I arrived at 10 a.m., enough time to meet Kim, have a look around, and hit some practice balls. The locker room may be the best I have seen so far. Tradition just screams out at you when you walk in. Its walls are lined with dark, old wooden lockers and pictures and placards that depict the history of the game in America. The names that surround you are Bobby Jones, Gene Sarazen, Sam Snead, Byron Nelson, and Ben Hogan. In fact, Seminole became Hogan's winter digs.

Kim introduced us to his friend Scott Probasco, a banker from Chattanooga, Tennessee, who would be our fourth. We met our caddies, and it was obvious immediately that they were professionals who work the likes of Shinnecock Hills, Baltusrol, and Pine Valley most of the year and come to Seminole for the winter. We were ready.

The wind was stronger than the previous day. The course is right next to the Atlantic Ocean, and there is a constant trade wind. Halfway down the first fairway Scott asked me about my quest and then asked, "Have you met a member at Wade Hampton yet?"

"No," I said. "Well, you have now," he politely drawled in his Southern accent. As you can well imagine, I quickly made note of that. It turns out he is also a member of the Honors Course in Chattanooga as well, but I had already played there. Scottie chipped in on Number 1 for birdie and apologized all the way to the second tee. "My real game will show up, just wait," he joked.

Kim is a jovial, cigar-chomping, opinionated guy, but always warm-hearted with entertaining stories. He spent many years as a USGA rules official, and I am doing my best to learn as much about the rules today as I can. Scott, however, told us an amazing story as we stood on the 4th tee, a par 3 of 161 yards. His wife had been a five-time Tennessee amateur champion and had played in the Curtis Cup. One day, years earlier, he and his three buddies were playing at Seminole, while his wife and her three friends played in the foursome in front of him. Number 4 is 141 yards for women, and the four women had a combined score of six. Think about it: two birdies and two holes-in-one. Scott saw the entire thing and says

LARRY BERLE   117

he heard one of the women who had scored birdie walking away from the green mumbling, "What do you have to do to win a hole around here?" The odds against such a feat are astronomical.

Number 6—a 383-yard par 4, slight dogleg left, heavily guarded by sand bunkers—was Ben Hogan's favorite hole in golf. He spent a lot of time at Seminole in the winters, according to Kim.

On Number 11, we ran into Billy Jo Patton, the only amateur ever to hold a lead at the Masters on the weekend. (He led after the second round and led again during the fourth, but a 7 at Number 13 halted his title hopes. He finished one stroke out of the playoff.) Kim introduced me as the "guy on the quest to play the Top 100," and he introduced Howard as the only Jewish American to ever play professional jai-alai.

You can bet the walls of Seminole's locker room have heard many great stories. When I tried to pay Kim for the guest fees and caddies, he whispered, "We don't like to see cash change hands here at Seminole. Send me a check."

heading toward the back 50

SAHALEE

Swinging at daisies is like playing electric guitar with a tennis racquet: If it were that easy, we could all be Jerry Garcia. The ball changes everything.

—Michael Bamberger

Sahalee, located in a suburb of Seattle, Washington, was designed by Ted Robinson, his only entry on the Top 100. Carved out of the tall cedar and Douglas fir trees that are native to the Northwest, Sahalee (which means "high heavenly ground") opened in 1969. In 1998, the course hosted the PGA Championship.

I got on the course with a phone call from the head pro at my club. Sahalee has reciprocating privileges with many clubs across the United States. I invited my friend Larry Hoof, who lives in Seattle, to play the south and north nines, which are the courses rated for the Top 100. As we crossed Lake Washington, we could see the home of Bill Gates being built on the shore. Massive is the word that comes to mind. It was a typical wet northwestern day, and even when it wasn't sprinkling, the course was soaked and produced no roll. It was an uneventful day, except for the fact that Sahalee was my 50th course. Next course I'd be on the back 50.

a golfer's dream

the east wing

CONGRESSIONAL

The difference between golf and government is that in golf you can't improve your lie.

—George Duekmejian, former governor of California

My friend Todd Peterson had a college roommate whose dad, Bill Brown, is a member at Congressional. Todd called Bill, and I was on. Congressional is in Bethesda, Maryland, a suburb of Washington, D.C., and was designed by Robert Trent Jones, Jr.

I assumed Congressional would be overrun with members of Congress, but I don't think that's the case (although I think it was the case when it was founded). There are two courses, East and Gold (go figure), and the list of golf-course designers who have worked on these two courses at various times is too numerous to mention. The East course is on the Top 100, and I met Bill Brown in the pro shop there. The course was not in very good shape, and from what I understand, that is often the case. Washington, D.C., lies in a transitional area as far as grass for putting greens is concerned: too far north for Bermuda and too far south for bent grass. Congressional was founded in the 1920s by two Indiana Congressmen as a place where Congressmen could play golf and entertain friends. Early members included John D. Rockefeller, Charlie Chaplin, and William Randolph Hearst. It has quite a list of past honorary members including at least half a dozen presidents.

The 1956 U.S. Open was played here on one of the hottest, most humid days in the history of the tournament. It was 100 degrees in the shade, and in one part of the course an official held a thermometer that read 115; Ken Venturi, the eventual winner, was in the clubhouse during the 45-minute break between rounds when Dr. John Everett examined him and advised him not to go back out. But lots of iced tea and a few salt tablets later and he was back at it. The great golf writer Herbert Warren Wind described Ken Venturi on the 18th green as follows: "His face was taut with fatigue and strain, and yet curiously radiant with pride and happiness." Venturi's struggle caused the USGA to abandon the 36-hole final day and extend the tournament to four days.

Congressional hosted another U.S. Open in 1997, and the final hole has become somewhat controversial. The USGA does not usually end its championships on a par-3 hole. But after studying all the various ways to change the order of holes to avoid that situation, the conclusion was that moving the crowds to support such changes would be impossible, and 18 was played last after all. Number 18 is a 192-yard downhill hole with water very much in play, and it turned out to be an exciting finishing hole for the Open.

two courses, one day

SAUCON VALLEY GRACE

ARONOMINK

As a musician you are always trying to touch the flame, get closer to perfection. So when you play something and Neil Young looks at you and says, "That's good!"—it's like you have attained a universal truth. And that's what a good golf shot is. At that moment, life is perfect. So of course you are going to keep doing it. It's insanely Zen.

—Graham Nash of Crosby Stills Nash and Young

I now had a mailing list of 125 people, and it was growing. The list included people who had hosted me, played with me, and helped me, and friends who were interested in being updated on my quest. And eventually, it had evolved from a mailing list into an email list. Early on, I sent out letters every three or four months the hard way: I typed them, copied them, addressed the envelopes, and mailed them myself. Now I wrote, spell-checked, and clicked "Send." Email made my quest much easier.

In a typical email, I wrote: "On Friday, I played two courses in the same day, Saucon Valley (the Grace Course) and Aronomink. Exhausting, but what a treat! Saucon Valley is in Bethlehem, Pennsylvania, about 60 miles north of Philadelphia. I was expecting a manger scene on the 18th green, but I had the wrong Bethlehem. The Grace Course is set in the foothills of the Poconos, and everywhere you look it's beautiful. I had a wonderful time playing with my cousin Andy Kneeter, my friend Barclay Douglas, and our host, Bill Leckonby. I was introduced to Bill through my friend in Carmel, Mike Assum. Bill is 79 years old, a former athletic director of Lehigh University, a great-grandfather, and he can still hit that golf ball plenty far.

"Two hours later, the three of us teed off at Aronomink, in the heart of Philadelphia. Barclay is a member there, so he arranged the time. Aronomink is another Donald Ross design, and the plaque at the first tee states, 'Donald Ross thinks this is his best work to date.' The course was in fabulous shape, although a few of the holes were undergoing renovations. The fairways now are mostly tree-lined, but that was not the case when Ross designed the course. I wonder what he would think if he saw this and many of his other courses today.

"There are only 47 to go on my Top 100 list now, and by the end of the year, I hope to be at 60 courses.

"On September 11, I turn 50 and I have a 50th-year celebration plan that includes adventure travel, spiritual growth, and physical challenge. It would take an entire letter to outline our plans, but in October we are going to Israel and Greece; in February, we are going to Africa and climbing Mount Kilimanjaro; and in the summer, we will go to Machu Picchu, Peru. The year will conclude with a hike to the bottom of the Grand Canyon and back. If you have a contact at any of the courses I have left to play, help is always appreciated."

Here are a few interesting additions to that email: Saucon Valley has three courses, plus a six-hole short course for a total of 60 holes. It was built by Bethlehem Steel Corporation primarily for its employees. The Grace Course is named for Eugene Grace, former president of Bethlehem Steel. It was designed by William and David Gordon in the 1950s. Aronomink, which was named after an Indian chief of the Lenape tribe, hosted the 1962 PGA Championship and the 1977 U.S. Amateur. The course plays to par 70 for men and par 74 for women; the distance issue was solved by adding par 5s for women.

sweet home chicago

MEDINAH

Medinah is a claustrophobia of trees.

—Alistair Cooke

I played Medinah with Cliff Wenz, whom I had met while playing at one of the Disney courses a year earlier. I'd seen pictures of Medinah's noble clubhouse, a gigantic Byzantine palace, but it was under renovation when I was there, so I never got to see the inside. Medinah is made up of three golf courses; Course #3 is its championship course. The club also has a pool, polo field, equestrian club, boathouse, skating rink, and a gun club—quite the complex. It was founded in 1925 for Shriners only, but after WWII, its membership dropped to such a low level that it began taking non-Shriner members. The clubhouse is said to be so opulent that some estimate it would cost $20 million to replace today.

Course #3 was originally designed as a ladies' course, but the ladies wouldn't play it because it was so long and hard. It was rebuilt in 1930 and failed again; in 1934, it was reopened a third time in its current configuration. In 1933 Medinah hired Tommy Armour as the club pro. Medinah lore claims that he used to amuse himself during dull lessons by shooting chipmunks with a .22 caliber rifle. One member, frustrated by Armour's neglect, asked, "When are you going to stop that and take care of me?" to which Armour replied, "Don't tempt me, you sonofabitch!"

Another Medinah story is often told about "Bud" Ward, who was near the lead after 36 holes of the 1949 U.S. Open. He stopped by the bar for a breakfast shot before the final 36-hole day. A friend joined him, and then another, and Ward kept drinking most of the morning and never made it to the first tee.

Course #3 has three tee boxes: 7,508 yards, 7,096 yards, and 6,776 yards. We played the short 6,776 tees (yeah right, real short). Course #3 is cut out of the woods, one long tree-lined hole after the other. It is lined with more than 4,700 specimens of oak and other species. Each tree is catalogued and labeled for type and age. The grounds crew anticipates the life of each tree and begins to grow a new tree nearby that will be maturing when its neighbor dies. Several hundred replacement trees are planted each year. Course #3 is challenging, but somewhat dull because most of the holes look alike and three of its four par 3s play at approximately the same length across the same Lake Kadijah (named in honor of Mohamed's wife). Of course, the fact that I shot 101 might have tainted my view somewhat.

the great lakes state

OAKLAND HILLS

I am glad I brought this course, this monster, to its knees.

—*Ben Hogan, winner of the 1951 U.S. Open at Oakland Hills*

Ben Hogan called it the "Monster" and the name stuck. Oakland Hills, located in a suburb of Detroit, Michigan, has two courses, North and South. That's probably about as much as you need to know about the North Course. In fact, that is all I know about the North Course—it exists. The South Course exudes tradition and history. The club was founded by a former Ford Motor Company executive and designed in 1918 by Donald Ross, who never saw many of the courses he designed. But Ross must have spent some time at Oakland Hills, because it's a masterpiece that regularly rates in the Top 10, and it clearly deserves the honor.

I'd been promoting some concerts around the United States with Kenyan singer Roger Whittaker, who is managed by Bruce Lahti. Bruce introduced me to Lincoln Cavaleri, who had just retired as the manager of Joe Louis Arena in Detroit, and he agreed to host me at Oakland Hills. He brought two of his sons, one of whom managed the Delta Center in Salt Lake City, home of the Utah Jazz. Right away I felt comfortable with this group, because we all knew a lot of show-business people in common and had many stories to tell about the shows we had promoted and the artists and agents with whom we had worked.

The Oakland Hills clubhouse is truly majestic. You'd never guess that the club's first pro shop was housed in a former chicken coup. Oakland Hills also has a prestigious tournament history; it has hosted six U.S. Opens, two U.S. Senior Opens, three PGA Championships, and one Ryder Cup. It is scheduled to host the 2008 PGA Championship. The legendary Walter Hagen was the first club professional. The 1951 Open, won by Ben Hogan, was set up with such great difficulty that it caused a change in USGA policy; from that point on, the USGA no longer permitted host clubs to control the course layout for an Open tournament.

The 1985 Open, the fifth Open hosted by Oakland Hills, was the scene for two very unusual events. On Number 8 of the first round that year, Tom Watson's putt hung on the lip of the cup. He waited until it finally fell, but according to the rules official, he had waited too long, and Watson was assessed a two-stroke penalty. At the end of the tournament, Watson was one stroke out of the lead, which precipitated a rules change. The allotted waiting time is now 10 seconds, and if you violate the rule, it's a one-stroke penalty, not two (a bit late for poor old Tom).

Another legendary Oakland Hills incident involved that same 1985 Open. T.C. Chen led all three days. He scored the first double eagle in U.S. Open history and tied the record low scores for the championship at that time after 36 holes (134) and 54 holes. On Sunday, things changed. At Number 5, he held a four-stroke lead. Then he double-hit his wedge shot from 30 yards off the green. It not only cost him a penalty stroke and a double bogey, but he lost his composure and fell out of the lead and eventually out of contention in the tournament. He lost to Andy North by one shot, and for a while T.C. Chen became known as "Two-Chip" Chen.

I didn't double hit and I didn't have any putts hanging on the lip. But I sure loved this golf course. It was in fantastic condition, and the holes were as beautiful as those on a parkland course could be. Number 16, for example, is a 400-yard par 4 with a pond at the front right of the green. It's a shallow green with a ridge running from front left to back right. An approach shot hit long to avoid the water will risk catching the back of that ridge and finding one of four bunkers behind this green. I shot an 88 that day and felt like I had brought the Monster to at least one knee. My 88 was the best of the foursome.

Rees Jones, one of golf's leading architects, is scheduled to redo the course to prepare for the 2008 PGA Championship. Watch for it. This course is definitely in my Top 10.

CRYSTAL DOWNS

A good golf course is not necessarily a course which appeals the first time one plays it, but one which grows on the player the more frequently he visits it.

—*Alister Mackenzie, course architect*

Alister MacKenzie, in my opinion, is the greatest golf architect to ever shape raw land into a golf course. He designed Augusta National, Cypress Point, Pasatiempo, Valley Club, and Crystal Downs, among others. He and Robert Trent Jones, Sr., are the only two golf-course architects to have been inducted into the Golf Hall of Fame. (Jack Nicklaus and Arnold Palmer are also in the Hall of Fame, but as players, not golf-course designers.) I had heard nothing but great things about Crystal Downs in Frankfort, Michigan, and I was looking forward to it with more anticipation than any other course on the Top 10 list.

My friend Dave Zubke has a law partner whose mother-in-law is a member at Crystal Downs. Dave called his law partner, Jim Diracles, who called his mother-in-law, and I had a golf date arranged at Crystal Downs. I flew to Grand Rapids, Michigan, rented a car, and began the long but beautiful drive to Frankfort. I pulled into a motel in Luddington, about an hour away, and when I woke up the next morning, it was raining. It was raining lightly but steadily, and it looked like a very slow-moving front. I put on my "optimist" hat, and I hoped beyond all hope that it would clear up. I also kept telling myself, "This is a beautiful drive, very calming and peaceful, through rolling hills and woods of Northern Michigan. Even if I don't get to play, this will have been worth it."

Finally I pulled up the entrance drive to the soaking wet, nearly deserted golf club on the shore of Lake Michigan. As I feasted my eyes on Crystal Downs, my thoughts of "beautiful day, beautiful drive, even if I don't get to play" went right out the window. "This place looks awesome and I really want to play here," I thought. The clubhouse is underwhelming, and the pro shop is simple and functional. Crystal Downs is all about the course, not opulent amenities, and it's one of golf architecture's relatively unheralded masterpieces.

I entered the pro shop and found a lonely pro behind the counter and Mary Weldele, my host. She was in her mid-60s and bubbling with energy and enthusiasm this dreary rainy day. I fully expected her to say, "Sorry you had to drive all this way, but please come back some other day," but she surprised me. "I actually like playing in the rain. Let's go," she said. "I have a cart with plastic rain sides on it, so we can stay dry." I got my clubs, and a few minutes later she pulled up in her cart, with no rain sides, wearing a baby-blue slicker and matching rain hat and looking like she was dressed for a fishing trip on the ocean. "Oops, the rain sides for my cart are in Florida. Sorry." What a trooper this woman was, I thought. It was still raining and showing no signs of letting up.

As wet as it was, I felt honored to have this wonderful golf course to ourselves. It brought new meaning to my idea of a "private golf club." We moved along quickly, but soon we were soaked through. After the sixth hole, Mary looked at me in despair and said, "I can't take any more. I'm drenched." As we were headed back to the clubhouse, I had very mixed feelings. I really wanted to finish, and I really wanted to get dry, but my feelings didn't matter. We were quitting. As of this writing, I have played one-third of Crystal Downs, but I will get back there to finish the course soon, and I can't wait. I know I am going to love this place in good weather.

carolina in my mind

THE OCEAN COURSE

I would have bent down on my knees and begged for the opportunity to build a course on such a magnificent property.

—Pete Dye, after he first walked the seaside land at Kiawah

I flew to South Carolina to play five rounds of golf in four days: the Ocean Course on day one, Belfair and Long Cove on day two (Belfair is not on the list, but it's a terrific Tom Fazio course), Haig Point, and, finally, Harbor Town. Not a bad week, eh?

In Scotland, there's a saying, "Nae wind, nae golf." Well, the wind almost always blows on Kiawah Island, home to the Ocean Course. The Ocean Course is one of approximately 20 Top 100 courses that are open to the public. You simply call to arrange a tee time, pay your money, and play away.

My friend Dave Zubke was attending a Wisconsin Bar Association meeting on Kiawah Island, and I tagged along. He played the first three courses with me before he went to his meetings. I represented him to the best of my ability after he left.

In *Bury Me in a Pot Bunker*, Pete Dye writes that because Kiawah Island lies east to west off the Carolina coast he was surprised to learn there is no prevailing wind. It blows alternately from the east and the west. Don't get that confused with "not much wind," however, because there is plenty of wind on Kiawah Island. Such a wind pattern significantly affects both length of holes and green sizes for golf architects, so this posed a perplexing problem for Pete Dye. He had to build larger, more receptive greens than he might have otherwise, and he had to build multiple tee boxes to allow for changes in hole distance depending on the wind. As a result, the length can be varied daily with a tee-box change. The greens are not similarly adjustable.

Until 1987, when Europe defeated the U.S. at Muirfield Village (which, by the way, was the first time the U.S. lost a Ryder Cup on home soil), winning the Ryder Cup was taken for granted in the Unites States. At no other sporting event save the Olympics is the American flag waved amid chants of "U.S.A.! U.S.A.! U.S.A.!" In August 1988, Pete Dye got a call from the PGA of America informing him that the 1991 Ryder Cup would be moved from the PGA West Stadium Course (Pacific Time) to Pete's proposed golf course on Kiawah (Eastern Time) to allow for prime-time television coverage in Europe. For the first time in history, this prestigious event had been awarded to a golf course that did not yet exist. The War by the Shore was incubating.

In July 1989, construction workers began clearing the land; in October of that year, Hurricane Hugo devastated the Carolina shoreline. Many of the trees and large portions of the sand dune were washed away; all vegetation was obliterated. Access roads were closed, so the construction crew had to take boats to the island. But the PGA didn't change the Ryder Cup's October 1991 tournament schedule. The press speculated that the course would never be in top condition. Adding to the construction delays, Pete's wife, Alice, realized that Pete "was building a course right next to the ocean but no one can see it." A high ridge of sand dunes blocked the views, so the fairways on many holes were elevated by six feet. Imagine what must have been involved in raising a fairway six feet!

The United States won the War by the Shore. The contest went down to the 18th hole of the last match, when Bernhard Langer missed a six-foot putt in his match against Hale Irwin that would have given him the point that Europe needed to retain the Cup. Following the Ryder Cup, the course would be played by resort guests from around the world, and Pete Dye had taken that into consideration in his design. The Ocean Course is laid out like a figure-eight, with the front nine looping clockwise along the salt marsh and the back nine looping counterclockwise while hugging the Atlantic shore. It may be the closest thing in the United States to true Scottish links.

The drive out to the course from Charleston on a heavily canopied, narrow and twisting road caused Dave Zubke to wonder if we were headed into a low-country ambush. When we arrived, it was spitting rain, which continued on and off for most of our round. Although the wind usually blows at Kiawah, it wasn't much of a factor that day, and everyone said how lucky we were. But I still thought the place was very hard. (The rain didn't help my attitude, I'm sure.) The tips play more than 7,700 yards, and the course recently had been overseeded (as it is every fall with grass that grows better in the cooler winter weather), so the greens and fairways were shaggy and slow. If you have never been in a waste area or waste bunker, then by all means visit the Ocean Course; there are hundreds of yards of them. I won't tell you my score—not because I am embarrassed, but because I blocked it out of my mind long ago. But by all means, you should test your golf skills here. (By the way, this is where The Legend of Baggar Vance was filmed.)

LONG COVE

If you are caught on a golf course during a storm and are afraid of lightning, hold up a 1-iron. Not even God can hit a 1-iron.

—Lee Trevino

We were in for more Pete Dye golf at Long Cove, but this course was a treat, even though I was a bit tired since it was our second 18-hole round of the day. Dave and I met our hosts, Tom and Judy Barth, had a quick bite to eat, and were off. The first hole had water all down the left side. Finally, on Number 4, we came to a hole without water directly in play. But that didn't last long. We soon discovered that water or marsh came into play on much of

Long Cove. Yow! Keep it straight!

As I have explained earlier, three or four times a year I would send an email to a list of nearly 150 friends and supporters. I had switched from regular mail to email and was glad of it. If I were doing this today, I would post a blog with photos and send out the blog address whenever I added an update.

The following email describes the Carolina trip after the Ocean Course:

"Designer Pete Dye has nine courses in the Golf Digest Top 100 and 11 (more than any other designer) on the Golf Magazine list. Long Cove is also a Pete Dye course, and it's located on Hilton Head Island, just down the road from Harbor Town. Unlike the Ocean Course, Long Cove is private and economically driven by its housing development, as are most new golf courses today. (Pete Dye said, 'I am like a kid with a lollipop,' referring to designing the Ocean Course without having to account for housing.)

Long Cove is long, narrow, and challenging with water in play on 12 holes. It plays like three different courses: tree-lined holes, almost desertlike holes, and holes with marsh and intercostal waterway. It's quite impressive. The houses are set back unobtrusively and the grounds are home to wildlife galore; it's a bit like walking through a bird sanctuary. I would love to return to play here one day when I am fresh."

HAIG POINT

The number one thing about trouble is don't get into more.

—Dave Stockton

The next day I played Haig Point, which I had arranged by calling the real-estate sales office and getting access to the course. I had to meet a realtor and listen to his pitch, and it was not only worth it but a learning experience as well. This was quite an adventure. Dave was attending his Wisconsin bar meeting, so I invited Tom Barth, my host at Long Cove, to play with me. He had played there before, but was glad for another opportunity to play the beautiful course on Daufuskie Island about a mile off Hilton Head. The island got its name, so the story goes, because it is the first in a string of "keys," or small islands, thus Da First Key.

The only way to get to the island is by boat, so we caught the 10:30 a.m. ferry and arrived at 11. The ferry carried a few passengers and several deliveries of groceries. There are no real stores on Daufuskie, just a small superette, so residents call the grocery store on Hilton Head, order what they need, and pick up the groceries from the captain at the ferry landing. Everyone drives golf carts (or takes the shuttle bus) because there are no cars allowed on this part of the island. How's that for a remote getaway?

We were on the course by 11:30 a.m., and it seemed like we had the place to ourselves. Apparently, no more that 25 to 30 rounds per day are played here, and there are few houses so it was tranquil and beautiful. Haig Point, designed by Rees Jones (son of Robert Trent Jones), is very innovative. There are several holes that wind their way through towering oak trees covered with Spanish moss, several forced carries over the tidal marsh, and a couple breathtaking holes on the ocean and intercostals. The course we played was Calibogue (pronounced Cali-bogey), which is actually two courses in one. The Haig course has several different tee boxes and fairways playing to the same greens, and there are actually two different holes for the Haig course as well. The course was in fabulous condition, and with the limited play it gets, it should have been. The day ended with 4:30 p.m. ferry ride back to Hilton Head. No doubt about it, our trip was a full-day adventure.

HARBOR TOWN GOLF LINKS

Harbor Town makes the player invent so many different shots you would think Pete Dye had stock in a third-wedge company.

—*Larry Mize*

I wrote in my email update to friends: "On Saturday morning at 7:54 a.m., I was at Harbor Town Golf Links—home of the MCI Classic and another Pete Dye course—on Hilton Head Island. I had heard from several locals that the course would be in terrible shape, and parts of it were, but most if it were, but most if it was fine. The day was overcast and rain was predicted, but as I stood on the first tee box, it was dry.

"I liked Harbor Town, especially the short par 4s. There are three holes that are 330 yards or less, and each of them offers a unique challenge. The overall length is only 6,500 yards (short by today's standards), with postage-stamp greens and very strategically placed trees and pot bunkers. I hit irons off the tee on these three holes and had only wedges in, but each approach had something very challenging about it, especially if I wasn't in the right spot on the fairway. Of course, walking up 18 was a thrill as I drove it to the right of the salty marsh and approached the famous red-and-white-striped lighthouse behind the 18th green. Every morning in South Carolina, I awoke to predictions of rain, but no rain fell until the 17th hole of Harbor Town, when it started raining and kept raining until I got on the plane at 5 p.m.

"Harbor Town brought my Top 100 total to 63. Of the 37 courses I have yet to play, I have connections at several and some are public access. I still need a connection for Peachtree and East Lake in Atlanta; the Country Club and Kittansett in Massachusetts; Shinnecock, Oak Hill, Garden City, and Atlantic in New York; and the Golf Club, Scioto, Canterbury, and Double Eagle in Ohio.

"In his book, Bury Me in a Pot Bunker, Pete Dye says Harbor Town is where his concept of small greens and a low-profile course was born. Some of his other signature ideas were born here as well: multiple tee positions, small- to medium-size 'shot-making' greens, undulating fairways, long waste areas, and abrupt, steep pot bunkers. Harbor Town is also where his signature use of railroad ties around water and bunkers was first implemented. Jack Nicklaus deserves some credit for the design of this course as well. He worked on Harbor Town with Pete Dye, and it was his first serious design project, well before he started his own firm."

the big networking payoff

GARDEN CITY GOLF CLUB

I owe a lot of my financial success in life to golf. Not just because of the money I won—in fact, that was the least part of it—but because of all the wonderful people I met who have helped me in so many ways.

—*Byron Nelson, golf's great ambassador*

Mike Assum, a friend of mine who lives in Carmel, California, volunteers for the Boys and Girls Club there. He introduced me to Donna Ferraro, director of Boys and Girls Clubs of Monterey. When Mike told her about my quest, she said, "I know someone at Garden City Golf Club. Is that on the list?" "Absolutely," I said. "I am a little reluctant because Garden City is an all men's club and I detest that," she said, but she called her friend, whom I will refer to as John, in New York City, and I was introduced to one of the most caring, giving men I have ever met. John holds a high-level position at a Wall Street firm, and when I called his office, he picked up the phone and bellowed out a warm greeting: "Hi Larry! I hear you are trying to play the Top 100. Well, I'll do anything for Donna, so tell me what I can do for you." Wow, I was bowled over. "I'm playing the Top 100. I've been working on it for five years, and I just finished my 63rd course. I have 37 to go. Donna told me you are a member at Garden City Golf Club and that you could help arrange for me to play there." "Consider it done," he said. "We'll go there together. When are you coming out and what other courses do you need to play while you are here? Shinnecock? The man at the desk next to me is a member at Shinnecock. I will get that one for you, too. How about Plainfield and Baltusrol? I can help there, too. And

137

have you played the four in Columbus? We have good friends at Double Eagle and the Golf Club." I was almost speechless.

On a good day, my past five years of networking had yielded one lead to one course at a time. My phone call to John was like striking oil. In fact, it seemed too good to be true. This man was offering me a way in to many of the places that are just not accessible to guys like me. His generosity was overwhelming, but I kept my composure until after I hung up the phone. I was in heaven, and I intended to make John my new best friend. A few days later, he called me back and we set a date for Garden City and Shinnecock. "Unfortunately I can't go to Shinnecock with you, nor can your host. I hope you don't mind playing there alone?" Yeah right, forget it!

Whatever fear I had of not being able to complete this quest was cleared away, at least for one day, by this phone call. Several times in the past few years, I had asked myself, "Am I nuts? This is impossible." And those feelings had grown in intensity in 1994 and 1996, when the list made its biannual change.

In May 1998, I traveled again to New York City, and again I had brought my golf clubs to my Cousin Liz's co-op in midtown Manhattan. I got up in the morning and went to Chelsea Pier, a sports complex on the west side of Manhattan with an amazing golf practice facility and a huge driving range at which you hit balls out over the river into nets. Score another one for the island of Manhattan. When I called John, he said he wouldn't be able to play with me, but everything was arranged; I should just go to Garden City on my own and find Jim Gilchrist, the general manager. I wanted to meet John, so I asked him if I could come to his office before I left. I brought him a copy of Golf in the Kingdom and a few other little gifts to show my appreciation. After a warm 20-minute visit, he was back to his trading desk and I was on my way to Garden City.

Jim Gilchrist greeted me at the clubhouse door and invited me to lunch. At lunch, he asked, "Do you want to play alone or with Joe and Tom who are eating at the next table?" I chose Joe and Tom over playing alone, and the three of us had a wonderful time together. After lunch, Jim gave me a hardcover book on the history of the club, which was founded in 1899.

There are three rules at Garden City: 1. No women; 2. Wear a sport coat in the clubhouse; 3. No cell phones on the course. That's it! Anything else goes. Word has it that no one cares whether or not you wear a shirt on the course.

Garden City is a terrific track, designed by Devereux Emmet. I don't know if he ever designed another golf course, but he did a fantastic job on this one. The signature of the course is the thick rough and the grassy mounds. Many tee shots demand forced carries of more than 150 yards, camouflaging hidden trouble and proper line of play. Garden City was built to spur growth of a model community, and it has hosted the 1902 U.S. Open, four U.S. Amateurs, and a Walker Cup.

Every hole was unique and memorable. The Travis Invitational, one of the New York area's major golf tournaments, was being hosted by Garden City the next week, and the course was being set up with high rough and fast greens to prepare for it. The rough was a real problem. I had a great front nine (5 over par) with several one-putt greens. The back nine was another story. I was in the rough too many times and ended the day with a 93. As I was leaving, I asked Jim if they ever allowed women at the club for special events. "We hold a dinner here once a year that the wives are invited to. We serve them in the parking lot," he answered. I'm sure they get a lot of participation in that! I got in my car and drove another hour-and-a-half onto Long Island to play Shinnecock Hills the next morning.

SHINNECOCK HILLS

Golf is good for the soul.
—Will Rogers

At 8 a.m., I was standing in the oldest clubhouse in America. Shinnecock Hills, named for the Indian tribe that once inhabited the land, is one of the five founding golf clubs of the United States Golf

Association. William Vanderbilt and a couple of his friends saw a golf demonstration in Great Britain and decided that golf needed to be introduced to the United States. They brought in Willie Dunn from Montreal to design a 12-hole course through the sand hills and underbrush overlooking Peconic Bay. In 1931, it was completely redone by William Flynn and Howard Toomey, who created its current look: striking ribbons of fairway spread through the windblown wild fescue grasses. Flynn designed three other courses on the Top 100: Cherry Hills, Cascades, and one of my favorites, Merion.

I was the only one there, save a couple employees. The sun, a massive orange ball, greeted me as it rose slowly over the end of Long Island. I took my time touring the locker room's photos and views and thinking of all the great golfers who have sat on these benches and used these lockers. The room had a magical feeling to it. I found the pro shop, met my caddie Bobby, and went to hit balls on the driving range. I am hitting balls where Arnie or Jack once stood, I thought. About a half-hour later another foursome showed up, so Bobby and I decided to get going, so as not to get in their way. I parred Numbers 1 and 2 and was hitting the ball quite well as we moved swiftly along the dew-swept fairways. Then, as we walked off the 8th green, Bobby turned to me and said, "These holes were just a friendly welcome to Shinnecock. Now the real golf begins." And so it did. From the fairway below, the 9th green looked like it sat up on a pedestal, and it was as hard to hit as it looked. Now I knew why the course was not just called Shinnecock. The hills of Shinnecock Hills were coming into play.

On the 10th tee, Bobby pointed well right of the fairway and said, "In the 1986 Open, this is where Jack Nicklaus lost his first ball in a competitive round." I did not lose my ball on 10, but I almost lost my composure instead. The green sits on a rather steep hill, about 50 feet above the fairway, and it drops off about 15 feet in the back, almost like a little island on a windswept hill. It runs steeply from front to back. I hit a short pitch shot over the back of the green. My chip shot coming back was a little hard and rolled off the green and down the hill 30 yards. With the next pitch I flew the green again and my chip coming back was a repeat of the first. If consistency was the key to golf, I'd gladly have taken inconsistency. I finally got it right the third time and sunk an eight-footer for my 11. "Are you doing this on purpose?" Bobby asked me. If it hadn't been so funny, I would have decked him on the spot.

The Number 11 tee box was a few steps away. Lee Trevino calls the 150-yard par 3 "the shortest par 5 in golf, because if you miss the postage-stamp green, you are probably going to make 5." I hit my tee shot into one of the four bunkers that are set approximately 15 feet below the green surface, then hit a great sand shot and walked away with four.

As we stood on the 12th fairway, Bobby said, "See that big mound on the left side of the green? You'll never see a pin over there, because there's a horse buried under there and it's sacred to the Indians." The course sits on the Shinnecock Indian reservation. When the club was founded in 1891, it signed a 100-year lease with the tribe. When I played there in 1998, its renewal was still unresolved.

Number 16 is a short 464-yard par 5, which may sound easy, but 24 of Shinnecock's 182 bunkers put a real premium on accuracy on this hole. When we were done with the round, Bobby and I headed back to the 10th tee and played 10, 11, and 12 again. Shinnecock Hills is a wonderful place and playing it alone was truly a magical experience. Imagine having one of the world's greatest golf courses all to yourself for a few hours.

In 2002, I had the privilege of playing the course again. I had completed my quest to play the Top 100 just down the road at Atlantic Golf Club. With Dave Zubke and Morgan Clawson, two friends from Minneapolis who were there with me, I played 36 holes the next day: 18 at Shinnecock and 18 just across the fence at National Golf Links of America. Now that's a great day of golf.

a golfer's dream

beautiful ohio

CANTERBURY

Golf is a game whose aim is to hit a very small ball into an even smaller hole, with weapons singularly ill-designed for the purpose.

—*Winston Churchill*

For several years my company produced the Twin Cities Beer Festival, where people spend an evening sampling approximately 150 different brands and types of beer. Stanley Stone was an exhibitor at the festival every year, representing a company that did quick glass-washing. After one of these festivals, I was leaving to play one of the Top 100 courses and I told Stanley about my upcoming trip. "Is Canterbury on that list?" he asked. "Why, yes, it is!" I said, as my ears perked up. "I have a friend, Dean Scherbel, who is a member at Canterbury, and maybe I can arrange a game for us there." It took some follow-up, but Stan came through and I had a game set up at Canterbury.

My longtime friend Bucky Zimmerman, a lawyer and great tennis player, had recently taken up golf. I invited him along on this four-day trip to play some golf with me. Bucky is an outstanding athlete and he was mastering the game quite quickly. He had never been on a "guys golf trip," so he was happy to join me. It was the first time that I had brought a friend along on one of my Top 100 trips, and I enjoyed the company.

We met Dean Scherbel at the Canterbury clubhouse in Cleveland. Canterbury, built in 1922, has been host to 13 major championships including two U.S. Opens, although we don't hear much about it today. The greens were in beautiful condition with very subtle and hard-to-read breaks. The front nine was the warm up to a hilly and exciting back nine with some great holes and elevation changes. Number 16 is a truly outstanding par 5 that meanders for 590 yards. Our caddie said that the elevation change from the 17th tee to the 18th green is the equivalent of walking up a seven-story building, but the incline is so gradual that you would never guess it.

THE GOLF CLUB

I don't know if this club is going to turn out financially in the red or the black.

—Developer Fred Jones, explaining his choice of red and black flags for the Golf Club

With just one phone call, John, my new best friend from New York, arranged a second trip for me to Muirfield Village and a round at the Golf Club with Woody Woodward, a car dealer in Columbus. Does John really know every car dealer in Columbus, Ohio? Hardly, but he's extremely well connected among golfers in cities all around the United States.

The Golf Club, rated No. 39 on the 2002 Golf Digest list, was founded in 1967 by Fred Jones. Rumor has it that Jones wanted to get into Scioto but couldn't get an invitation, so he decided to build his own club and hired a virtually unknown Pete Dye to design it. Today Pete Dye is a world-renowned golf-course architect. Back then, he had designed only one course and was working on his second, Crooked Stick, in Indianapolis, Indiana. Jones really went out on a limb to hire Dye, and his risk paid big dividends.

Fred Jones had a vision and was not about to be deterred from it. The Golf Club was to be a private sanctuary in which his friends could play golf and cards whenever and however they wanted. He slowly acquired 400 acres (a lot of land for a golf course), most of which was signed over to him on crumpled handwritten notes and napkins he kept in his pocket. When one of his friends asked him if he'd had surveys done on the land, he retorted, "Of course not!" In the end, he turned all his notes and agreements over to a real-estate attorney who put everything in order for him.

Bucky and I had just played Canterbury, in Cleveland, with Dean Scherbel. I called our host, Woody Woodward, to see if there was room to bring Dean along with us. He said, "Sure," so Dean played with us. On the way to the Golf Club, we passed the estate of Les Wexner, owner of the Limited and one of the most influential businessmen in Columbus. I later learned that in this little 65,000-square-foot shack, the main dining room (there are several) seats about 20. The table sits on an elevator, which lowers to the kitchen below, where place settings and meals are set up, then raises back up to the dining room. What a way to have your meal served to you?

The Golf Club caters to its members. It's available whenever a member wants to use it, seven days a week, 365 days a year. The club has 150 members. Why 150? "We only have 150 lockers," is the stock answer. Women are not banned, but there are no women's tees or locker rooms, and women are allowed to play only at designated times. The clubhouse is very simple, with a tiny pro shop and a luncheon area adjacent to the spacious locker room with its imposing portrait of founder Fred Jones. The Golf Club had no head pro until recently because, Jones claimed, "No pro can make a decent living here, not enough lessons. Our members will take their lessons at their home clubs."

On beautiful days, Fred Jones was often heard to say, "If you can't play golf on a day like today, you have a damn poor job." When those beautiful days come along, it's easy for members to get in a round of golf at the last minute: Just show up and tee off. The Golf Club has no tee times, which is not hard to manage with a membership of 150.

A couple of Pete Dye's signature design elements may have first appeared here: A coyote skull lies in a waste bunker on the second hole, and until last year a hangman's noose hung from a tree near the 16th hole. The noose was removed after one of the grounds crew was mowing the grass close to the creek. His riding mower lost traction, slid down the steep embankment, turned over, and pinned him face down. He drowned in 16 inches of water. The noose was taken down out of respect.

Four hundred acres should be more than enough for any golf course, but there was something about Number 12 that looked unfinished to Pete Dye. He asked Jones to purchase six acres across from the 12th tee. Fred Jones fulfilled Dye's request without even batting an eye. The fact that the Golf Club was completed at all is a tribute to Pete Dye. At one point during its construction, Fred Jones fell ill and spent some time in the hospital. After several days, Dye visited him to report on his progress. "Haven't you run out of money, Pete? Do you need more?" Jones asked. Pete responded that he had run out of money several days earlier and taken out a personal loan to continue the work on the course. Talk about trusting your employer!

Many years ago, the Golf Club and the USGA talked seriously about moving the USGA Headquarters to the Golf Club property. It would have been quite a coup to get the USGA Headquarters to move to Ohio. Then one day a USGA official casually said to Fred Jones, "We will be mighty proud to host the U.S. Open here." Suddenly, all negotiations were off. "I built this club so my friends can play anytime they want," Jones said. "I am not closing this club down to members for three weeks to host an Open." And that was that.

Bucky Zimmerman, Dean Scherbel, and I met Woody Woodward at the clubhouse. Woody, who owns a Chevrolet dealership in Columbus, was excited to host us, show off the Golf Club, and hear about my quest. Golf junkies love to talk about golf. The Golf Club is a difficult course, make no mistake about it. The fairways are tight, the greens are severe, and the terrain is rugged. Although the fairways and greens are in terrific condition, the surrounding woods look natural. I shot a 94, respectable for a tough course like this, and birdied Number 15. Woody (an 11 handicap at the time) shot an 81. People have said that I'm easy to play with, which might be why I've been witness to many personal-best rounds. Woody was certainly happy with his performance that day.

SCIOTO

I still feel that one of these days I'm going to be like Rip Van Winkle and wake up and find it's been a good, long dream.

—*Byron Nelson (but this could just as easily be said by me)*

The next day, Bucky and I headed for Scioto Country Club. Scioto is the oldest club in Columbus and renowned as the place where Jack Nicklaus grew up. We played with Pete Reiber and Jim Kennedy, who is a lawyer (like Bucky) and also president of Scioto. Playing with the club president is definitely a bonus. Scioto is an excellent course in beautiful condition with many uneven lies and small well-protected greens. A creek running through the property brings water into play on many holes. It's a great place to play golf.

Scioto, designed in 1916 by Donald Ross, would have little notoriety outside of Columbus were it not for the fact that Jack Nicklaus grew up playing golf here. Scioto has hosted the 1926 U.S Open (which was won by Bobby Jones), a 1931 Ryder Cup, and a 1950 PGA Championship. According to Robin Obetz, who played lots of golf with his close friend before he turned pro, this is where Jack learned and perfected his high fade. He was already one of the longest hitters in golf, with perhaps the strongest pair of legs as well, and extra distance was not a consideration for Nicklaus. Accuracy and control were his priorities.

All the places that cause golfers the most trouble at Scioto are on the right side of the fairway, making it an unlikely course on which to perfect a fade. Nicklaus warmed up before playing and then headed right to the practice tee after each round for a truly concentrated practice. His work ethic was unflagging. Not only did he spend hours practicing after each round, he spent weeks practicing after the season ended. Throughout the winter, Jack and Robin would take a heater out to the small hut next to the snow-filled driving range and hit balls until they ran out. The balls were collected when the snow melted. Scioto is also where Nicklaus was introduced to his longtime teacher, Jack Grout. And rumor has it that Nicklaus played his first nine holes ever here at age 10 and shot 51.

a golfer's dream

please come to boston

SALEM COUNTRY CLUB

On November 4, 1895, 12 of Salem city's most distinguished citizens, intrigued and for the most part uninformed about a game with Scottish origins called golf, met at the old Salem Club, today known as the John Bertram House on Salem Common, to organize the Salem Golf Club.

—Gary Larrabee

Boston boasts two Top 100 courses: Salem Country Club and the far more well known Country Club. I stayed in the city with Barclay Douglas and his family. I played Merion and Pine Valley and a couple other courses with Barclay when he lived in Philadelphia. He had recently moved and now lived in the Boston area, but unfortunately, he couldn't play either golf course with me.

The golf pro at Bearpath, where I am now a member, called the pro at Salem Country Club and arranged for me to play. I wish it was always that easy. Barclay lives on the southwest side of Boston; Salem lies on the far north end of Boston. Salem is legendary as the town in which people accused of practicing witchcraft had been burned at the stake, therefore the club logo is a witch on a broomstick.

Salem Country Club was designed by Donald Ross. I'm usually not a big Donald Ross fan, but there are two or three of his courses I really like and Salem is one of them. Ross must have spent a lot of time here, because the course has a terrific layout and is fantastically manicured. I was teamed up with Buzz Martin and Larry Templeman, both retired and in their late-70s. The course was deserted but for the three of us and a couple of foursomes. The U.S. Senior

Open was scheduled to take place at Salem in 2001 and someone from the USGA was out on the course taking photographs. Larry and Buzz played from 5,800 yards, hit it nice and easy, and were a hundred yards down the middle all day. I played from 6,500 yards, and they both marveled at how far I hit the ball. I glowed a little inside each time they commented on the length of my shots because I'm usually the shortest hitter in my foursomes. On the third hole, Larry said, "I can't take a longer backswing because my arm hits my pacemaker." We got around in about three hours. We were joined for lunch by four members of their regular golf group, all retired except one. He was 91, still practiced law, and played golf two days a week. He was a real inspiration to me. I hope I am still playing golf at age 91. I shot 87, including a 9 on Number 15. Don't ask; I've blocked it out.

THE COUNTRY CLUB

There is nothing as exciting in golf as playing for your country.

—Byron Nelson, former Ryder Cup player

The next morning I was off to play the storied and historic Country Club. No nicknames here; the Country Club is its full name. Founded in 1893, it is one of the oldest courses in the United States and one of the five founding courses of the USGA.

Bart Osborn, a friend in Minneapolis, is also trying to play the Top 100, but he seems less intent than I was on reaching that lofty goal; he just wants to keep playing great courses (not a bad gig if you can get it). Bart's cousin, Ed White, is a member at the Country Club. Tall and handsome (he looks like Robert Redford), Ed was my gracious host. The Ryder Cup was to be played at the Country Club almost one year to the day after this round, and Ed was in charge of the corporate village. Every tent and ticket had been sold and every volunteer slot was filled, so there was no invitation or opportunity for me to attend. But I was thrilled to be on the course. Coincidentally, my friend Evan Schiller was also here taking photographs of the course for the PGA of America. The Country Club has also hosted 13 national championships, including three U.S. Opens.

The design of the course is credited to Willie Campbell, but Ed told me there was a committee of members who worked closely with Campbell and had significant influence on the design. There are three nines here, the Championship 18, and the nine-hole Primrose course. The Open course on which the major championships are played, and thus the course that is rated by Golf Digest, is a bizarre hybrid of the two courses. According to Ed, a member's wife suggested incorporating the Primrose course into the layout to be used by the U.S. Open in 1963. As I remember it, the 12th hole of the Open course is the 8th hole of the Primrose course, and the Open's Number 13 is the Primrose's Number 9. Number 11 is a composite of a par 4 and par 3. So I couldn't play this layout if I had wanted to because it does not exist except during an Open.

You might be interested to know that the 1913 U.S. Open, the subject of the book (and movie) *The Greatest Game Ever Played*, was played at the Country Club. Francis Ouimet, a 20-year-old former caddie who lived across the street from the Country Club, beat British greats Harry Vardon and Ted Ray in an 18-hole playoff for the U.S. Open Championship. It was significant not only because of Ouimet's background, but because his was the first victory by an amateur in an Open.

It was very windy (two to three clubs of wind) the day I played the Country Club, but I had an excellent front nine. I shot 40, followed by a 46 on the back for an 86 on the day. Then Ed showed me the card from the course record held by Peter Jacobson: a 64 with 30 on the front including a string of seven straight 3s. Suddenly my 40 didn't look so good anymore.

The Country Club appears to be a small village of yellow clapboard buildings with white trim. It has a traditional looking clubhouse and locker room. It has a guardhouse but no guard; it does, however, have a stuffed uniform sitting in the guardhouse that at first glance looks like a guard. I don't know if this is intended to have the "scarecrow" effect or if it is someone's idea of a joke. I found it hilarious.

a golfer's dream

two steps forward, one step back

SHOAL CREEK

My design ideas change with every course I do, but I believe all my thinking came together at Shoal Creek.

—Jack Nicklaus, course designer

At the beginning of my quest, I tried to play as many of the Top 75 as possible, thinking that they would be most likely to stay on the list longer. My assumption was accurate, but sometimes an opportunity came up to play one of the last 25 and I took it. When Golf Digest came out with its biannual Top 100 list in May 1999, 12 new courses came on the list. Of the 12 that were dropped, I had played seven; of the new ones on the list, I had played one, World Woods, for a net loss of six. Before the issue came out, I had 26 courses left to play. Now I had 32. It might take a bit longer to achieve my goal, but if I have to play more great golf courses in the process, well, that's not much of a burden for me!

With this in mind, Annie and I traveled to Alabama to play some courses on the Robert Trent Jones Golf Trail. While we were in Birmingham, we played Shoal Creek. Kim Whitney, who got behind my cause toward the end and helped me with some contacts at several courses, introduced me to Glen Ireland, who is a member at Shoal Creek. Make no mistake about it, this is the South and this club is very Southern.

Shoal Creek hosted the 1984 and 1990 PGA Championships; the 1990 Championship brought notoriety to the club that it much rather would have avoided. A month before the championship, Hall Thompson, founder of Shoal Creek, stated in an interview that black members would never be admitted to his club. "That's not done in Birmingham," he said. Civil-rights leaders threatened to picket the championship, and major advertisers pulled millions of dollars from the telecast sponsorship. It quickly became a national issue, and soon the PGA and USGA announced that no future tournaments would be held at clubs that discriminate. Shortly thereafter, Shoal Creek invited a black member to join, and Augusta National recruited a black member prior to the 1991 Masters. According to Thompson, recruiting black members at that time was a challenge. Very few blacks could afford the initiation, he said, and of those who could, not many wanted any part of the place.

Shoal Creek is a wonderful Jack Nicklaus design cut from a rich forest cradled in the lap of Oak and Double Oak Mountains at the southern end of the Appalachians. It features towering pines, dogwoods, azaleas, and a meandering creek and feels a lot like Augusta National.

Annie and I played with Glen Ireland and his daughter Nonnie. Glen was a 12 handicap at the age of 73. A year earlier he shot his age and was damn proud to share that with us. We had a family match: Glen and Nonnie vs. me and Annie. My family got its butt kicked, but isn't that what good guests should do? Glen is the only person I've ever met who'd played golf with Bobby Jones. He was a friend to Bobby Jones' son while they were in college, and the three of them played several rounds of golf together. This man was so kind he invited Annie and me to spend the night at their home. Now that's Southern hospitality!

BALTUSROL

Reading greens here is like trying to read a book printed with invisible ink.

—Anonymous

Baltusrol has to be the only golf club that got its name from a murder. Murder victim Baltus Roll was the original owner of the farm on which the golf course now lies. The club was founded in 1895 in New Jersey, just a few miles from New York City. In 1918, A.W. Tillinghast was hired to design two courses (the original course was buried). Tillinghast was a very prolific designer; only two architects, Robert Trent Jones and Donald Ross, have had more courses on the Top 100.

Baltusrol holds a cherished place in golf's rich history. It has hosted 16 national championships. The giants of golf have walked its fairways for more than a hundred years: Bobby Jones was here. So, too, were Walter Hagen, Gene Sarazen, Ben Hogan, Byron Nelson, Sam Snead, Jack Nicklaus, Arnold Palmer, and, of course, Tiger Woods. Talk about Founding Fathers! Even George Washington maneuvered troops over this land during the Revolutionary War. Baltusrol has the distinction of being the only 36-hole facility to host a U.S. Open on both its courses. Jack Nicklaus won two of his four U.S. Opens on the lower course (the one I played). Even with such an illustrious history, Baltusrol isn't nearly as well known as places like Shinnecock or Pebble Beach.

One reason for its relative anonymity may be the club's membership. Baltusrol's founder was quite a promoter, getting the club in the spotlight whenever possible. When the club was sold to its membership, staying out of the spotlight became the goal. Larry Carpenter, a longtime member at Baltusrol, remembers as a teenager being paired with Stu Baker, who at the time was chairman of Chase Manhattan Bank. Larry asked him what he did for a living, but Stu didn't seem to want to tell him. After Larry pressed him, Stu said, "I work for a bank." That speaks volumes about the culture at Baltusrol. People just want to be golfers when they are here.

Baltusrol is not a course with many memorable holes. It has no ocean, lake, or mountain range to frame it. Rees Jones said it perfectly: "You may not remember a lot of the holes, but you remember they are interesting and challenging to play." Even Lee Janzen said, "It's strange, but I went back after winning the U.S. Open there, and I didn't remember all of the holes."

There is a memorable story about the clubhouse burning down on March 27, 1909. One philandering member arrived at his Manhattan home early in the morning on the 28th and told his wife that he had spent the night at Baltusrol. Without a word, his wife handed him the paper with the story of the fire on the front page. Caught redhanded!

Prior to the 1954 Open, Robert Trent Jones was hired to "strengthen" the course. He was heavily criticized for the severe par-3 Number 4, which played over the largest body of water on the course. But he silenced his detractors when he first played the hole. Jones struck his tee shot into the hole for an ace. "Gentlemen, the defense rests," Jones said. "I think the hole is eminently fair." The 1954 U.S. Open marked two firsts: the first Open to be nationally televised and the first Open to use gallery ropes to cordon off the fairways.

My friend John had set me up to play with his colleague Bob Lecky. I drove out to Baltusrol from New York City with plenty of time to spare, but a north turn on the freeway rather than a south turn took me 15 miles out of the way, and suddenly I was late for my 1:30 p.m. tee time with Bob. The first person we saw was New Jersey Nets coach P.J. Carlisimo, just a few months after he had been choked by one of his players. After we hit a few balls, Bob and I and our caddie were off. The caddie's dad had been a career caddie at Baltusrol, and he had been there eight or nine years himself, so he knew the place like the back of his hand. I needed it, too. The breaks of the greens are clearly affected by Baltusrol Mountain, and the greens are very tricky with extremely subtle, hard-to-read breaks. As helpful as my caddie was, I had a poor score, but it was a fun day overall. I took some pictures of us (which I sent to the caddie later) and gave Bob a copy of Golf in the Kingdom. The clubhouse, by the way, is like a USGA history museum. Fantastic!

barnstorming

SAND HILLS

When I first saw this land, I knew it was the golf architect's opportunity of a lifetime.

—Bill Coore, golf-course architect and design partner of Ben Crenshaw

Developer Richard Youngscap spent much of his youth in the sand hills of Nebraska. In 1991, he bought 8,000 acres of those sand hills with the dream of building a golf course. He hired Ben Crenshaw and Bill Coore to design the course, and when Sand Hills Golf Club in Nebraska debuted on the Top 100 list, it was the talk of the golf world. Golf fanatics will travel to the middle of nowhere to play an outstanding course.

Sand Hills is private, but when I played the course, limited outside play was allowed. The club's first head golf professional was Jim Kidd, who was the pro at Interlachen in Minneapolis before moving to Mullen, Nebraska, to take the job. I didn't know Jim Kidd, but we knew several people in common, so I called and asked him what I had to do to play Sand Hills. "Send a letter stating when and why you want to play the course and who would be playing with you," he said. "The committee that considers such requests will get back to you."

My friend Todd Peterson in Minneapolis had introduced me to Jeff May, a pilot with a small four-passenger plane. One day they decided to find a place within a couple hundred miles of Minneapolis to fly and play golf and at the last minute invited me to fly along. I didn't have to think twice. Our first trip was to Giants Ridge in northern Minnesota. Todd, Jeff, Ron Fingerhut, and I had a blast together and decided to do it again. They quickly designated me as the guy to find the good courses in a 200- to 300-mile radius and arrange to play them. It was a job I knew something about, and this assured me that I would be joining them. After a couple of these relatively short trips, I suggested that we play Sand Hills. They were all over that idea, so I sent a letter to Jim Kidd. Early in the summer of 1999, I got a phone call saying my request was being honored.

Sand Hills is all about the golf. "Golf courses are built for many reasons," Bill Coore said over lunch months later. "The main ones are demographically driven: to support real-estate development or public play and, in some cases, purely for golf. Bandon Dunes and Sand Hills are two leading examples of the pure-golf scenario.

"Dunes land is the foundation of golf," Coore continued. "This is the land that golf architects like me look for: wind, sand base, random contours on the land. Sand Hills was site-driven not demographically driven. It was built for the sake of golf and for no other reason. It's a place where millionaires can play next to local rancher members. Golf has its deepest roots in this kind of land."

When they first looked over the site, Crenshaw and Coore say they "discovered" 130 natural holes of golf. Their job was to pick the best and most routable 18, which they did. Why here? According to Youngscap, "Some of the best golf courses are discovered not created. The abundance of pure water and superior sand were two other key factors that figured into their decision."

When Sand Hills was developed, the average cost to build one green to USGA specifications was $40,000, which includes contouring and creating the sand base so that the grass grows properly, accepts shots properly, and drains properly. The draining quality of sand hills is equal to or better than USGA specifications for a green, so drainage-system costs were not an issue. The average green at Sand Hills cost $3,000, less than 10 percent of the average green at that time. Rough-grading costs were also minimal: $7,000 compared to hundreds of thousands on most golf courses. Only 2,000 cubic yards of dirt were moved to create the golf course; Tom Fazio has moved more dirt on a single hole. Eighty-five percent of Sand

Hills' construction was eaten up by the irrigation system.

Ron, Todd, and I flew with Jeff in his plane to North Platte, Nebraska, arriving at 4:30 in the afternoon. We headed north on Highway 97, a small two-lane highway surrounded by sand hills as far as the eye can see. The road was deserted; we saw five cars in the hour it took to get to mile marker 55. Yup, you've got it, there's no sign that reads: "Sand Hills Golf Club Next Left"; we were directed to turn at the dirt road one-tenth of a mile past mile marker 55. Blink at 60 miles an hour, and you miss it. We drove three miles down the dirt road, and just when we all thought we had made a wrong turn, the clubhouse appeared almost like a mirage.

Play is limited to 60 to 80 players per day at Sand Hills. Most members stay in the club's 20 cabins and play an average of 36 holes a day. Other than golf, only four activities are available: eat, drink, play cards, and sleep. The evening we spent at the clubhouse felt like a night at camp, according to Todd. We checked in to our modest but very comfortable accommodations, jumped into our gas golf cart (Sand Hills uses gas carts due to the distance between the clubhouse and the golf course), and headed for the practice putting green under an expansive Midwestern sunset.

We had an excellent dinner and were up at the crack of dawn the next morning. It was a mile-long ride to the course, where there is only a driving range, starter shack, and lunch shack. "We wanted the experience to be as purely golf as possible," Bill Coore explained. "No man-made buildings, no noise or visual pollution. That is why the clubhouse is built away from the course. We even considered a private airstrip (there was plenty of land), but we didn't want the noise pollution. We wanted everyone's experience to begin in North Platte, so they could experience the rolling hills of the Midwest all the way up the highway. To some people, it's a brand new experience."

The course terrain is rolling, with fescue surrounding the fairways and hardly a tree in sight. It was calm and hot when we started and very windy when we finished. As we ate lunch outside, it was a challenge to keep our food from blowing off the plates.

Jeff, Todd, and I all agreed that there are no memorable holes at Sand Hills, but the experience is one that we'll never forget.

Our caddie, Brett, was a high-school senior from Mullen, the nearest town, 20 miles away. "Do you play golf?" Jeff asked. "Yes sir, I am a four handicap," Brett quickly replied. Brett also mentioned that he had a girlfriend. "What do you do on a date in a town with a population of 554?" Jeff asked. "We spend lots of time visiting with her parents," Brett answered. No wonder he had a 4-handicap.

VALHALLA

How lucky can a guy get to be able to play a game all his life and then be able to take that game and put it on a piece of ground to last the rest of his lifetime and many more people's lifetimes. That's pretty special. I've had a pretty special life and been a pretty lucky guy.

—Jack Nicklaus, course architect

The trip to Sand Hills really piqued Jeff May's interest in playing more Top 100 courses with me. "A private pilot is always looking for an excuse to fly somewhere," Jeff said. "So I was thrilled when Larry invited me to play some of the Top 100 courses. Who in their right mind would turn down an opportunity like that?" I was thrilled to have a friend along and excited to travel to some of them in a private plane. Jeff's four-seat plane flies approximately 200 miles per hour (about 40 percent of the speed of a commercial jet). It can fly into airports that are very close to the golf courses and move from course to course very efficiently. More important, it's fun. I'm licensed as a glider pilot (no engine), so I appreciate learning more about flying, and the experience is exciting.

One call from my pro and we had a tee time at Valhalla, the site of the 1996 PGA Championship. It took us about three hours to fly to Louisville, Kentucky, where we got a courtesy car from the airport and drove to the course. The PGA of America has bought a substantial interest in Valhalla, so it has several major championships to its credit, including the 2000 and 2004 PGA Championships and the 2007 Ryder Cup. Designed by Jack Nicklaus, Valhalla has a beautiful variety of holes and some very challenging greens—too challenging, according to my friend Jeff.

DOUBLE EAGLE GOLF CLUB

May thy ball lie in green pastures, and not in still waters.
—Ben Hogan

The next morning Jeff and I flew to Columbus, Ohio, in his plane. This was the way to go, I thought, except when Jeff had to give wide berth to some thunderstorms as we took flight from Louisville. Looking directly into a thunderstorm from a small airplane is a little nerve-racking. My life was in his hands, and he did a great job.

You may remember that there are four Top 100 golf courses in the Columbus area; the only other city in the world to hold that distinction is Melbourne, Australia. The last of the four Columbus courses on the Top 100 was Double Eagle. Our trip was arranged by my friend John from New York who called the Double Eagle pro and got us on. This course is distinct from the other three in Columbus. And unlike the Golf Club, it is perhaps the best manicured course that I have ever stepped foot on.

We met assistant pro, Gary, in the clubhouse and went out to hit balls on the range. "Just let me know when you are ready to go," he said. A few days earlier, Gary had hosted another person playing the Top 100 named Bob McCoy. Bob was on a journey to play the Top 100 in the world in 100 days. What an amazing accomplishment!

There was no one else around when we warmed up and met Gary in the pro shop. As we walked out the main door of the pro shop, we found ourselves in a carpeted tunnel where the members' clubs and carts are kept. (You don't want to get exposed to the elements too soon!) Our clubs were placed on a cart. As we rode to the first tee, Gary said that Double Eagle has 223 members, but only one-fourth of them live in Columbus, so the course is never busy. A typical day here means 50 to 60 rounds of golf, only 6,000 rounds a year. By comparison, my home club gets 6,000 rounds in five to six weeks. What a shame that such a beautiful course gets so little use! Even though there is rarely anyone else on the course, you must wear long pants to play here, no matter what the temperature. Double Eagle isn't the first club where I have come across the long-pants rule, but it's rare.

Double Eagle was developed by John H. McConnell, and it is ruled by a committee of one (as is the Golf Club). Mr. McConnell is often seen around the club wearing a golf shirt with "The Committee" embroidered on it. Members join by personal invitation of Mr. McConnell. There is only one house on the golf course. Guess who it belongs to?

Double Eagle is known for its superior condition, and I would wholeheartedly agree with that assessment. It felt like we were walking on plush carpet for 18 holes. The greens are true and quick. There are no traditional tee markers; you just walk up to the yardage plates and hit from there. If the turf is a bit worn, you move forward or backward a pace or two. Double Eagle was designed by Tom Weiskopf, a Columbus native, and Jay Morrish, and there are some wonderful holes here: a couple across lush ravines and a couple with double fairways or distinctive alternate routes to the green. Another feature at Double Eagle is Number 19, a playoff hole for matches tied at the end of 18. Weiskopf and Morrish were a fantastic design team, and I wish their partnership had not dissolved. I was very happy with the 89 I shot that day.

Gary shared an interesting story on the 17th tee, a 355-yard par 4: Head pro Don Shimko scored a hole-in-one on 17, the only hole-in-one in his life and the only double eagle ever scored at the Double Eagle Golf Club. The dues structure at Double Eagle is also a bit unique. There are no monthly dues, just one bill at the end of the year after the year's expenses are tallied up.

I don't say my golf game is bad, but if I grew tomatoes they'd come up sliced.

—*Arnold Palmer*

After the round at Double Eagle, Jeff and I flew to Latrobe, Pennsylvania, home of Arnold Palmer. We landed at the Arnold Palmer regional airport, just east of Pittsburgh, and saw Arnie's jet parked nearby on a runway. He had landed just 30 minutes before us and was long gone. We drove to Ligonier, 15 miles from the airport and about 10 miles from Latrobe, where Arnold Palmer lives.

I met Howdy Giles through my friend John in New York City. Howdy is a dentist who lives in Wilmington, Delaware. He's not only Arnold Palmer's dentist, but he identifies himself as Arnie's biggest fan. Several months earlier, John had asked me to get six good seats for Lion King in New York City (at the time a tough ticket), which I did through some of my theater connections. It turned out these tickets were for Winnie Palmer (Arnie's wife) and their grandchildren. That transaction had started with John, but I ended up in communication with Howdy. Not only did he offer to host me at Wilmington Country Club, but he also offered to get me on Laurel Valley, which he did by calling the head pro Curt Siegel, a close friend of Arnie.

Jeff and I drove to our hotel to check in, and we weren't in the room 10 minutes and the phone rang. "Good afternoon, Curt Siegel here. How was your trip in?" "Great," I said, hardly believing my ears. If that wasn't surprising enough, he asked, "Can I take you guys to dinner?" "Well, yeah." We met him at the clubhouse and hopped into his car. "Feel like a good steak?" he said. "Sure." We drove until Curt pulled off into the empty parking lot of what looked like a house. Curt walked up to the door, rang the doorbell (the front door was locked), and we were greeted by the owner and welcomed into the restaurant. I've never found out the name of it, nor do I know whether this was business as usual. I do know the three of us and one other table were the only customers, and the owner came and went from our table like he was family. Wow, what an experience! Curt made us feel like royalty from the moment we landed until we walked off the golf course the next afternoon.

We showed up at Laurel Valley at 7:30 a.m., and Curt was walking out to meet our car as we pulled in. He set us up at the range and then took his post at the first tee, greeting all the members and their guests as they teed off. It was just Jeff, me, and our caddie Brian. Brian was a 4 handicap and had caddied for Arnold Palmer dozens of times. He'd even played a few rounds of golf with Arnie. He was a great caddie and made a special day even more special. On the 6th hole, Curt came by in his cart to make sure everything was going all right. Talk about service!

Jeff and I both fell in love with Laurel Valley, which is set in the foothills outside Pittsburgh. This piece of land was a golf course waiting to happen. The immaculate course is more about discovery of great holes than about creating great holes. Laurel Valley easily makes my Top 10, but unfortunately, or maybe fortunately, the course gets little notoriety among golfers, especially compared to Oakmont, its neighbor 40 or 50 miles down the road. Laurel Valley's membership is corporate, and the club has terrific guesthouses, fantastic food, good meeting space, and awesome golf. We had lunch with Curt, who introduced us to Sandy, Arnie's sister.

Like many great golf courses, Laurel Valley is the vision of one man—George Love—and it's a testament to his unrelenting drive for excellence. Arnie lives 15 miles from here at Latrobe Country Club, where he grew up and his dad was the greens keeper, but Arnie plays Laurel Valley quite a bit and is a serious presence here. Jeff and I went by Latrobe Country Club and checked it out before we returned reluctantly to the airport to fly home. I was exhausted. I don't know how Jeff stayed awake all the way home, but I did my best to stay up with him so he didn't fall asleep.

georgia on my mind

EAST LAKE GOLF CLUB

East Lake stands as a symbol of tradition and honor to those who know its history and were a part of its past. But, even more importantly, it stands as a symbol of hope to future generations.

—Anonymous

Born in 1902, the great Bobby Jones grew up in Atlanta, Georgia. He won five U.S. Amateurs, four U.S. Opens, and a Grand Slam in 1930, and was without a doubt the world's greatest amateur golfer. Jones grew up playing golf at East Lake Golf Club, a wonderful Donald Ross design. His father, Colonel Robert T. Jones, served as club president for five years. At the age of 13, Bobby defeated his father in the final to win the club championship. Over time, East Lake deteriorated dramatically. The clubhouse fell into disrepair, the club fell from popularity, and the neighborhood around East Lake became dangerous and blighted. In 1993, East Lake was bought by Tom Cousins, who completely renovated the clubhouse and the course, and turned the clubhouse into a tribute to Bobby Jones. Tom Cousins' renovation became a cornerstone of the redevelopment of the entire East Lake neighborhood.

Only corporations can join East Lake and the initiation fee is $250,000; $50,000 goes to the club and $200,000 goes to the East Lake Community Foundation, including the East Lake Junior Golf Academy (which serves mostly inner-city and minority kids). The Academy introduces golf to kids who might not otherwise get exposed to the game, and it has had great success in achieving its mission. It is a worthy mission that more golf-course developers should adopt. I served on the board of the Fairway Foundation in Minneapolis, which is also dedicated to introducing golf to inner-city and minority kids. Fellow board member Dan DeMuth introduced me to an old friend of his who was the events coordinator for the Tiger Woods Foundation. He called Sam Puryear, the executive director of the East Lake Junior Golf Academy, and Sam was my host at East Lake.

As I approached the course in my rental car, you could see that the club and surrounding grounds had a spanking new look that contrasted with a neighborhood in transition. The more I learned about how Tom Cousins had used this club renovation to turn around this neighborhood, the more impressed I became. Bobby Jones grew up across the street from the 13th tee box, and I had my picture taken in front of his house. I was hoping that standing in front of his house would cause some of his skill to rub off on me, but that didn't happen. The clubhouse is a tribute to the great Bobby Jones and worth a trip all by itself. East Lake now hosts the Tour Championship every year. Watch it on TV.

PEACHTREE GOLF CLUB

It was a good day for bad golf.

—*Jeff May*

I sent the following email to my friends after I played Peachtree:

"It seems to be a Bobby Jones weekend. But then how could it be anything else, since Atlanta was the man's home. It is another glorious day in Atlanta. I am staying in a northern suburb, socially and economically about as far from East Lake as you can get. Peachtree's membership consists of the longstanding blue-blood families of Atlanta, so exclusive I could find no sign on the front gate whatsoever.

"My friend Bart Osborn, who serves on the board of directors of the Fairway Foundation with me, has arranged today's game with Asa Candler VI. Asa comes from a very prominent family in

Atlanta. His grandfather created the formula for Coca-Cola and founded the Coca-Cola Company.

Peachtree was designed by Robert Trent Jones. It is one of his first courses and jump-started his career as a golf architect. And guess who worked on the club with him? Bobby Jones (no relation), the founder and first president of Peachtree. Jones is credited as co-architect of the course, just as he is credited with co-designing Augusta National several years later. Peachtree looks and feels like Augusta, with similar rolling terrain and vegetation. You may be interested to know that the clubhouse, the old Samuel House Plantation House, served as General Sherman's 1864 headquarters in his march through Atlanta to the sea.

"I played poorly. I shot 97, Bart shot 87, and Asa shot 82. Asa had invested some money in a company that was going to sell a new 'driver' concept via infomercial on the television. It had a magnet directly behind the clubface and the magnetic field was supposed to aid in moving the ball farther and straighter. He had several versions of these drivers in his bag, and Bart and I tried them several times throughout the round. I didn't notice anything miraculous about them, nor did Bart, and I never saw them on the market either. Today makes 78 courses that I have played so far, with just 22 to go.

"As I looked over the Top 100 list on the flight home, I realized I had reached close to 80 percent of my goal. Then I looked at the 22 I had yet to play and asked myself, 'How am I ever going to pull this off? I've been trying for years to find someone at these places.' Still, I felt a real sense of accomplishment and I told myself, 'You can't quit now!'"

a golfer's dream

the oregon trail

BANDON DUNES

Build it and they will come.

—Field of Dreams

Those of you who followed this list closely know that Bandon Dunes, which is ranked Number 41 in the 2001-2002 Golf Digest List, was not even on the list in May 2000 when I first played there. There was a buzz about Bandon Dunes from the day it opened, and I had heard many good things about it. So when I sent my letter out that spring, I said, "I am sure that some of you are asking why I am writing about Bandon Dunes when it is not on the Top 100 list. To that I say, 'Not yet!'" A golf course must be three years old to qualify for the Golf Digest Top 100 list, and Bandon Dunes was barely a year old. It was awarded the best new upscale public course in 1999, and as soon as it was eligible, it was on the Top 100. When it appeared on the list, it really boosted my confidence: I know a great course when I see one.

Mike Keiser developed Bandon Dunes. In 1991, his nationwide property search led him to Bandon, Oregon, a small town in southern Oregon on a remote stretch of land sitting high on the bluffs overlooking the Pacific Ocean. This wonderful piece of coastline is home to seabirds in flight and men fulfilling their golf dreams. "I wasn't interested in commercial golf," Mike Keiser said in an interview in Golf Connoisseur, "I was interested in dream golf. When I built Bandon, I wasn't sure anyone would come."

But golfers come from far and wide to play golf in this special place. I headed there for a Shivas Irons Society weekend golf event, which was centered on golf and meditation and how they relate to golf and life. My golf game had gone to hell (handicap up six strokes in the past year), and I faced many of my anxieties related to my rising handicap square in the face. It was helpful, painful, enlightening, and sometimes ugly all wrapped up in one weekend.

We played two rounds in two days in all four seasons of weather. After each round, we had group discussions about the emotional journeys we took in our minds as we played. Mine were all over the place, from fear and anxiety over bad shots and, even worse, anticipated worse shots, to being awestruck by the course overlooking the Pacific Ocean. On the plus side, I was with friends whom I had not seen in a while and I made some new friends as well.

Bandon Dunes feels like a Scottish links course, as well it should. It was designed by an unknown Scottish architect named David Kidd (his father was golf-course manager at Gleneagles in Scotland). Kidd insisted that the clubhouse be built inland, saving the coastline for the golf course. (Rumor has it that this was a big factor in Kidd's hiring; the other architects all recommended giving the clubhouse an ocean view.) In fact, when David Kidd showed up for his interview and saw the formidable lineup of well known golf architects he was competing with, he was ready to pack it in and head back to Scotland. Thinking he didn't stand a chance of getting the job, he went to the interview with a list of conditions, such as the clubhouse's inland location, no homes or buildings on or near the course, and the feel of a traditional "British Isles" links course. He left feeling sure he would never hear from the club again, but a couple of weeks later, Mike Keiser called to say, "You're hired."

"God as golf architect" with David Kidd doing the routing, but Bandon Dunes is magnificent. It has six wonderful holes on the ocean, with gorse, heather, rolling hills, and plenty of sand dunes. It is a walking-only course, so be prepared to walk and be prepared for some breathtaking views of the Pacific Ocean.

The clubhouse and adjacent lodge and sleeping rooms are understated but perfectly suited to their surroundings. The food is excellent. There is nothing here but golf: If you eat, drink, and breathe golf, you are going to love it. A second course, Pacific Dunes, designed by Tom Doak, was under construction when I played Bandon, and a third by Ben Crenshaw has now been built as well. Pacific Dunes has made the Top 100. When asked why they are both so highly rated, Mike Keiser said, "The ocean is certainly an important element. If these were inland, I doubt they would have the same appeal. Also, they are public. Most of the best courses built in the past 40 years are private. It's rare that a really good public course gets built."

SUNRIVER RESORT & CROSSWATER GOLF CLUB

Don Quixote would understand golf. It is the impossible dream.

—Jim Murray

Bandon is on the southwest coast of Oregon near the town of North Bend. Bend is in the middle of the state; as the crow flies it's about 175 miles from North Bend, but no highway takes you across the Cascade Mountains. I was told it would take six hours or more to drive there. I called a private airplane charter company in Bend and asked how much it would cost to have someone pick me up in Bandon in a two-seat plane. The flight was about one hour and 15 minutes and the cost about $250. A commercial flight, changing planes in Portland, would have cost nearly as much and taken most of the day. I had the plane pick me up the next morning. The plane was a single engine that flew approximately 125 miles per hour, and the pilot often flew as part of a fire watch for the forest service. This being timber country, I learned a lot about tree planting and forestry. As we flew, you could see the forest in various stages of growth from the youngest to the oldest that were almost ready for harvest. Not only did I learn a lot, I enjoyed the beautiful flight through the Cascade Mountains. We landed in the next valley, just a few hundred yards from the Sunriver Resort. They gave me a ride to the resort (saved a rental car), and I checked into my room and headed out to play golf.

Designed by Bob Cupp and John Fought, Sunriver Resort was ranked as America's best new resort course in 1995 and debuted at 89 on the Golf Digest Top 100 list. The high-desert course sits in a valley of forested meadows and preserved wetlands surrounded by the Cascade Mountains; the Deschutes River threads its way through the course several times. The snow-covered peak of Mount Bachelor always seems to be in view. The course is also a wildlife habitat and in 1999 it was named a member of the Audubon Sanctuary Program, one of only 150 courses in the U.S. at that time to be awarded that distinction.

Crosswater plays up to 7,683 yards (the longest course I've ever seen) with par 5s of 582, 635, 687, and 598. I did not play those tees, but even from my tees, these were cripplingly long par 5s. There was hardly anyone around, so I played alone, which was a nice break from the past two days when I was with large groups of people. I had been playing poorly, and I faced some of those demons on this round. When I hit bad shots, I just dropped another ball and hit until I got it right. Leisurely soaking in the beauty of this course was a wonderful solitary experience. I shot 91, which wasn't bad, and I had a chip in, a couple sand saves, and most impressive to me, an up and down from a bunker 125 yards away.

As I sat in my room that evening, I realized I had only 19 courses to go. It would be so much more fun to finish, I thought, if my game would come back. I thought not only about dropping my quest, but dropping the game altogether. Then I came to my senses. Like the guy who has a terrible day on the course, so terrible that he is at the locker-room sink slitting his wrists, when one of his foursome walked by and casually asks, "Are you playing with us tomorrow?" As he quickly covers his wrists with towels, he responds, "What time?"

doodyville, u.s.a.

WILMINGTON COUNTRY CLUB

It's Howdy Doody Time.

—*Buffalo Bob Smith*

Howdy Giles lives in Wilmington, Delaware, near Philadelphia, so I flew into Philly to meet my new friend. As I mentioned, I was introduced to Howdy by John in New York. Howdy is Arnold Palmer's dentist and touts himself as "Arnie's Number One Fan." He's collected thousands of pictures of Arnie and has had some memorable experiences with the master. Arnie even came to his son's wedding. When John asked me to get Broadway tickets a few months ago, it turned out to be for Winnie Palmer and her grandkids via Howdy Giles. Howdy thanked me by hosting me at Wilmington. I met Howdy and his wife in the clubhouse for lunch and discovered we had much in common. We have a mutual friend in Minneapolis, Kim Whitney, who really stepped up to the plate to help me get on several courses toward the end of my quest. Howdy also is a member of the Shivas Irons Society, and we had plenty to discuss about golf as a metaphor for life and my experience at the Golf in the Kingdom Workshop at Esalen. Howdy gave me an autographed copy of Arnie's biography, a great read.

Howdy had many Palmer tales to tell. The best story was about the day Arnie shot a hole-in-one with him at Wilmington Country Club; Howdy told it as we stood on the 13th tee where it happened. (It is one of 17 holes-in-one that Palmer has had in his career.)

As you might guess, Howdy is a big Howdy Doody fan, and a few years ago he played a round with Buffalo Bob Smith, who led every show with, "Hey kids! What time is it? It's Howdy Doody time!" Howdy visited Bob's house and had his picture taken with the original Howdy Doody puppet. I don't think he met Clarabell, though.

My golf game was still on vacation, and I did my best not to let it get me down. So my round at Wilmington was all about relationships and being the most entertaining guest I could be. Telling my Top 100 stories and listening to Howdy's Arnie stories was so much fun that I can barely remember the golf course.

rocky mountain high

THE SANCTUARY

You're only here for a short visit. Don't hurry, don't worry. And be sure to smell the flowers along the way.

—*Walter Hagen*

In July 2000, I returned to Colorado to play the Sanctuary, in Sedalia. New on the list since I had been here, the Sanctuary is located about five miles from Castle Pines and is constructed on very similar terrain: high in the mountains with lots of elevation changes. I brought along my friend Bart Osborn and we played Castle Pines again. I didn't play as well this time, but what a treat to be able to play such a fabulous course a second time and the Sanctuary. A friend of Bart's had arranged for us to play Castle Pines. Getting on the Sanctuary was my doing.

The Sanctuary has no members and no public play. So, how exactly do you arrange to play the course? The Sanctuary's owners, Dave and Gail Liniger, are founders of RE/MAX Realty. Why not just call Dave Liniger and ask if you can play in his backyard? I called the clubhouse (yes, there is one) and told the pro what I was trying to do. (At that point, I had played 82 of the Top 100.) The pro said Mr. Liniger hosts five or six RE/MAX events a year for his top-performing employees and that Mr. Liniger donates the course for charity events 15 to 20 times each year. "I can fax you a list of upcoming charity events and you can sign up for one of them," he said. There was a range of events from $200 to $1,000. I called the Colorado State Highway Patrol to sign up for the Chiefs Challenge Charity Golf Tournament, which was the cheapest and most con-

175

venient date for me. I was faxed an application, I sent it in with my money, and Bart and I were in. I still don't know exactly what this charity does, but if Dave Liniger is prone to speeding on Colorado Interstates, his annual donation probably gets him some preferential treatment.

We showed up at 9:30 a.m. on a crisp morning, met our playing partners, Stan Mickelson and Randy Van Oren, and entered the putting contest. Wow, these are some interesting greens. In the mountains, prevailing wisdom tells you that all putts break toward the valley but, in this case, it was hard to determine which valley. There were valleys everywhere. At 11:30, we were off to the 17th tee, our starting hole today, and suddenly we were experiencing the shock and awe of the Sanctuary. I was glad our foursome had been assigned a forecaddie so someone could help me read these greens.

Dave Liniger hired a little-known golf architect named Jim Engh to design the course. Engh did such a fantastic job that the Sanctuary debuted on the Golf Digest list at No. 45, one of the highest debuts in the history of the rankings. I recently spoke with Jim Engh who said that three golf architects had looked at Mr. Liniger's land prior to his interview for the job and all three had said, "It's impossible to build a golf course here." Jim Engh saw opportunity where others saw only obstacles. He explained that golf course architecture for him is about the golfing adventure. He uses intrigue and interest to create memorable, unique holes. "If you finish playing a golf course and say, 'Oh, I get it!' that's not for me," he explained. We talked about Number 8, which is one of the few holes with an uphill shot to the green. They dug a bowl into which they dropped the green site and contoured the green so you can see the green surface from the fairway below. If you have played severely uphill holes, you can imagine what a challenge this is. Normally, you can only see the top of the flagstick. Jim Engh has designed several courses and won many accolades.

From an aesthetic point of view, the Sanctuary may be the most beautiful I have been on to date. The highest point on the course is 6,590 feet; the lowest point is 350 feet lower. Fourteen of the 18 holes play downhill, and quite a bit downhill at that. From nearly every green you climb to the next tee. Thank God for golf carts. The club has had its golf carts modified for more power and added a more extensive charge for the batteries, because you are always riding up hill.

Number 1 is a 574-yard par 5, with the lush green fairway laying 185 feet below the cliff that is home to the first tee. I felt like Superman when my 3- wood carried 265 yards.

The Chiefs Challenge tournament's format is a modified scramble. Everyone hits a tee shot, we picked the best of those, and everyone played their own ball in from there. Our team came in second. I got closest to the pin on Number 6. Bart eagled Number 4, a 535-yard par 5, and Randy eagled Number 8, a 300-yard par 4, knocking it in from 90 yards out on the fairway. I shot an 84 for the day. Not bad.

There is no real-estate development around the Sanctuary (real-estate development is what economically drives many of the golf courses being built these days), so there wasn't a home in sight, not a human home at any rate. There's forest as far as the eye can see: scrub oak, towering pines, rugged outcrops, and plenty of wild animals including black bear, elk, mountain lions, and eagles. On one of the holes, we saw two wild turkeys walking across the fairway. Oh, and did I mention four waterfalls?

As you would expect in a charity tournament we had to wait on lots of tee boxes, but who cares when the views of the Rockies are so spectacular? As we stood on the tee box at Number 5, one of the highest on the course, you could see Pike's Peak in the distance in one direction and it seemed like you could see all the way to the Wyoming border in the other.

At the banquet following the event, I met Mr. Liniger briefly and found out that he and his wife donate a foursome for 30 or 40 charity auctions each year. I went home and wrote a letter asking him to donate one to the Fairway Foundation, and the next year my friends and I bid on it and won. On my second trip, I took along three friends and got to see their awestruck reaction to the views. This time we had the place almost to ourselves and I got to play my own ball for the entire round. After we left, my friend Todd Peterson realized he had left his sunglasses on the cart, but we were outside of the closed gate. No one answered the call box, so Todd climbed the gate and went to the cart barn to get his sunglasses. That's private!

SOUTHERN HILLS

Hazards attract; fairways repel.

—*Thomas Mulligan, for whom the mulligan was named*

Jeff May and I took off on another of our fly-and-play Top 100 golf course adventures. We were planning to play four courses: the first being Southern Hills, the site of the 2001 U.S. Open and the last Oak Tree in Oklahoma City with Tony Greenberg, a friend of Barclay Douglas. When Tony heard we were playing Southern Hills on this trip, he asked if he could join us. So I called David, our Southern Hills host, and he agreed to add Tony to our group. I had been introduced to David by Don Knutson through his friend Bill in Omaha. It was a convoluted process, but I was on and happy about it. We met David in the clubhouse, spent about a half-hour on the range, and headed for the first tee.

Southern Hills has hosted 13 major golf championships, including the 1958, 1977, and 2001 U.S. Opens and the PGA Championships of 1970, 1982, and 1994. That's a whole lot of championship golf for a small city like Tulsa, Oklahoma. Southern Hills was funded by oilman Waite Phillips (Phillips Petroleum). Founded in 1936, it is one of only two golf courses to be built in the United States during the Depression, when golf courses were closing across the country by the hundreds.

Perry Maxwell designed Southern Hills, and he excels at making a course look easy and play hard. The course was rated No. 25 on the Golf Digest list. During the summer of 1999, just two years before the club was scheduled to host the U.S. Open, Southern Hills' greens were vandalized. Using strong herbicides, vandals spelled out profanities against the newly hired greens superintendent who had just fired most of the greens crew. What a welcome, eh? My planned trip to Southern Hills that summer was abruptly cancelled when the course was closed from August 1999 until June of 2000 (although there were still nine holes that members could play). Holes were lengthened; bunkers and greens were rebuilt. In fact, the par-5 Number 5 was lengthened to 615 yards in order to "Tiger-proof" it, but several guys got there in two during the Open anyway. Tony and I went back and tried to play it from 615. He made a six; I made a nine.

Not only did I not break 100, but I got so frustrated with a shot from a fairway bunker on Number 12 that I slammed my 6-iron onto the ground, a rare occurrence for me. As luck would have it, it struck a sprinkler head and busted the club head right off the shaft. After the embarrassment washed over me, we all had a good laugh (really, what else can you do?). Fortunately, I didn't need a 6-iron again on that round.

Southern Hills has Bermuda grass fairways and greens. The greens are overseeded in late fall, and the Bermuda fairways were dormant when we played the course. The grass looked dead and ratty. During the 2001 U.S. Open, which was played in the blistering heat of summer, the fairways looked green and lush as I watched Retief Goosen 3-putt from 12 feet on the treacherous 18th to blow his lead in the final round. He held off Mark Brooks in an 18-hole playoff the next day for the win. We went back to the airport, hopped in Jeff's plane, and flew to Fort Worth.

COLONIAL COUNTRY CLUB

The toughest par-70 in the world.

—*Dr. Cary Middlecoff*

We landed in Texas around sunset and stayed with Todd Schreiber, a friend of Jeff's who lives near the Dallas-Fort Worth airport. The next morning we were off to the Colonial Country Club in Fort Worth. We were playing with Brock Stephens, who was introduced to us by Todd Peterson. Todd is a friend of ours from Minneapolis. Brock is the husband of Todd's wife's college roommate. (And that sentence is a fine example of the intricate web of relationships that got me on some of these courses!) A fine Southern gentleman, Brock couldn't have been nicer. He was not only welcoming, but very interested in my quest and how it was going. He is not a member at Colonial, but he is very well connected in the golf world, and we were playing Colonial with him today.

This club is the home of the annual Colonial Invitational. Annika Sorenstam played against the men here and just barely missed the cut. (I'm sure you read about it—it was covered ad nauseam.) Most important, Colonial was the home course of the legendary Ben Hogan. The Hogan room on the first floor of the clubhouse is filled with memorabilia, photos, trophies, and even his old locker. It's an awe-inspiring place to ponder the likes of Hogan walking these halls. A wonderful statue of Hogan overlooks the 18th green, leaving you with one last reminder of the great one before you retire to the clubhouse.

Brock Stephens is an outstanding golfer. He once placed 11th in the Texas State Amateur, and 10 years ago he won the California State Long Drive Contest with a drive of 361 yards. Brock opened the round eagle, birdie. He had a two-foot eagle putt on Number 1, and on Number 2, he hit the flagstick from the fairway. He went on to shoot even par 70 for the day.

Colonial is a great test of golf. It is dominated by rows of dense trees on almost every fairway, and the player who is able to control the shape and trajectory of his shots will do well here. I had barely gotten warmed up on the front nine when I came to "The Devil's Horseshoe" (Colonial's version of Amen Corner): Numbers 3, 4, and 5. In 1983, Tour Magazine called Number 5 the toughest par 4 on the PGA tour. Cary Middlecoff had this to say about it: "First I pull out two brand-new Wilson balls and throw them in the Trinity River. Then I throw up. Then I go ahead and hit my tee shot into the river." Number 5 is a 470-yard par 4, with the Trinity

River running up the entire right side of the fairway. It was Brock's only bogey on the front nine. I made seven.

The course was designed by John Bredemus in 1933; Colonial is the only course he designed, as far as I know. Its putting greens are seeded with a new strain of bent grass called A-4, bred to withstand Texas summer heat. I was doing very well in Colonial's greenside bunkers—up and down three of five times—and ended the day with a 94, better than I had hoped for. I was happy. We had cool weather, and it even sprinkled on us a couple of times.

After the round, Brock gave me a SeeMore Putter. (He had an affiliation with the company.) According to Brock, SeeMore Putters have been used in 10 PGA wins, including Payne Stewart's U.S. Open win at Pinehurst. I fell in love with the putter and carried it in my bag for five years. It has a straight shaft and a red dot on the putter head directly below the shaft. When you address the ball, make sure that the red dot is hidden from view every time. That way the loft and face angle are always the same—simple but ingenious.

The next day we were planning to fly Oklahoma City to meet up with Tony again and play Oak Tree, but there were tornadoes in the area. Jeff and I decided to head for home before severe weather hit, and we had a clear, safe flight back to Minneapolis. When the Top 100 came out again, Oak Tree had fallen off the list, so I lucked out. Eighty-seven courses down and 13 to go—I am getting so close I can taste it.

a $500 winning bet

SHADOW CREEK

A good golf course makes you want to play so badly that you hardly have the patience to change your shoes.

—*Bernard Darwin*

I know that feeling of anticipation well. In 1989, Shadow Creek (now rated No. 20) debuted at No. 8, the highest debut in the history of the Top 100. The course was dreamed up by casino guru Steve Wynn and designed by Tom Fazio. If Shadow Creek doesn't prove Tom Fazio's design genius, I don't know what does.

For the first few years of the club's existence, the only way onto Shadow Creek was via a personal invitation from Steve Wynn. He reviewed the tee sheet daily, and if he disapproved, you were immediately removed. How was I going to get on the course? A personal letter to Steve Wynn? Hmmm. In 1995, I promoted a Smothers Brothers concert in Minneapolis and played a round of golf with Tommy Smothers at my club. He said he'd played Shadow Creek. You can be sure that I asked if he could help me get on, and he said, "We used to play his casino every year. Then they stopped hiring headline entertainment, so we got a job at another casino. I called the head pro and asked if I could play when I was in town. The pro said, 'You've played here before. I don't see why Mr. Wynn wouldn't invite you back.' But the next day, the pro called me sheepishly and said, 'Mr. Wynn has denied your request, so I don't think I can help you.'" His story set me back a little, but I still wondered what I could do to get on.

A few years later, Annie and I were in Cabo San Lucas and some-

183

one yelled her name as we were walking down the sidewalk. It was an old friend from Minneapolis who was on vacation, staying with Lyle Berman. Lyle manages many Indian casinos and owned the Stratosphere in Las Vegas. We all ended up at dinner that night. When I asked Lyle if he could help me, he said, "Probably. When Shadow Creek is your last course, call me and I will call Steve Wynn for you."

Then the situation at Shadow Creek changed. The story goes that the IRS came to visit Steve Wynn and told him that the expenses for the course were not legitimate business expenses. This is not a business, the IRS said, this club is for your personal friends. "Okay," said Wynn, "it's now open to the public for $1,000 per round." I really did not want to pay $1,000 to play Shadow Creek, or any other golf course for that matter, so I just tucked the information away and forgot about it. In 1999, Steve Wynn sold the golf course and a couple of hotels. The new owners priced a round of golf at $500, plus the cost of a room at Treasure Island, Bellagio, Golden Nugget, or Mirage. I booked an $89 room at Treasure Island.

It was a chilly day at Treasure Island with Jeff May and my long-time friend from Seattle Larry Hoof (we played Sahalee together) who came to Las Vegas just to share this day with me. We had a good dinner and avoided big losses in the casino. The next morning we were picked up by a stretch limousine and taken to Shadow Creek. The limo was part of the $500 fee, as was the caddie. The only vehicles allowed into the club are those of delivery services, employees, and hotel limos. What a way to arrive at a golf course! The front gate was guarded, but the guards waved our driver through.

Once the limo pulled out of the city, nothing disturbed the flat, wide expanse of desert except Shadow Creek as you approach it. You see fence, you see trees completely lining the perimeter of the course, and finally the gate. In contrast to its desert surroundings, the course is an oasis of rolling hills, framed by glistening brooks, ponds, and waterfalls, and mature stands of trees, all shaped into a golf Mecca that looks a lot like northern Minnesota.

I picked up a coffee-table book about Shadow Creek with two photographs on the front cover. Both pictures are of Steve Wynn and Tom Fazio. In one, the background is bone-dry flat desert; in the other, the background is a green framed by a waterfall, a pond fronting the green, and hundreds of trees. It looked like it was cut out of lush rainforest. The caption notes that these are before and after pictures taken in the same exact place.

"I had to be convinced to take this job," Tom Fazio writes in the book. "When I am approached to design a golf course, I am invariably told by my client, 'I have a great piece of land.' When I first met Steve Wynn, we stood on a flat, barren piece of desert, and he said, 'You have a blank canvas. You can create anything you want,' I realized that I had never had this kind of opportunity before, but it also scared me to death. I was fascinated by Steve's sense of design. I submitted routings and finally the usual clay model. Steve wanted a bigger model; in fact, he wanted it three times bigger. Steve also wanted to see the course from the perspective of a six-foot-tall golfer walking all 18 holes. So we pasted in pictures of the mountains in the background of our model and moved a crane-operated fingernail-sized video camera from tee to green on every hole of this model."

"Tom Fazio had many concerns before taking this job," Steve Wynn writes in the book. "I am sure he doubted my resolve to see it all through, once all the costs were tabulated, so I gave him a broad understanding of the economic factors and the impact of international tourism in Vegas. The large-scale model was ultimately the bridge that brought us together. Shadow Creek's primary objective was to excite one's emotions and secondarily, test one's golf skills. I didn't care how tough it was; I was more interested in what kind of an experience the golfers would have [which may be why the USGA was never invited to rate the course for slope and rating until the new owners took over]. The use of shadows, in this sunniest of states, was a very large part of the design element, creating visual texture. Water features were kept small and recessed."

A 200-acre bowl the size of the course was dug out of the desert to create the perimeter of Shadow Creek. Except for the surrounding mountains, you cannot see over the rim. You'd never know there is a desert out there. Thousand of mature trees, more than 21,000 by the time they were done, were imported and transplanted. "I had intended to seed the course and sod some of the steep hillsides," Fazio said. "Steve Wynn, however, wanted a solid playing surface opening day, so we sodded the entire golf course. In all my years, it had never even occurred to me to do this."

Unfortunately, we had a cloudy day at Shadow Creek, so the shadows that are a large part of the design were not in play. Larry, Jeff, and I were picked up by the limo at 10 a.m. Yeah, baby! All three of us were greeted by name as we stepped out of the limo at Shadow Creek. We entered the elegant clubhouse, were assigned lockers labeled with celebrity names, and were off to the practice area. The practice area should not be confused with a driving range. It is divided by stands of trees into areas that hold four people each, so your group can practice in privacy. (God forbid that Michael Jordan should look over and see us.) Everyone hits to the same set of targets. What a concept. We had an 11:30 tee time but were told we could go whenever we were ready. There was one foursome out on the course, and a pair of twosomes scheduled to play around lunchtime. We checked the scorecard to determine which tees we were going to play. There were only two choices: 7,239 yards and 6,701 yards (women have it tough here). It was an easy choice for us, and we were off on our adventure.

We were on a car with our forecaddie. I hit the opening tee shot right up the middle that is virtually enclosed by pine trees with Shadow Creek cascading up the left side of the fairway. With the snow-covered peaks in the distance, you hardly notice it is a dogleg left. We did notice all the wildlife: owls, ducks, reeves, ringnecked pheasants, rabbits, widgeons, mute swans, and even a pair of black trumpeter swans—abundant would not describe it, overthe-top might. Finally, I asked the obvious question: "How do you keep all these animals here?" "We feed them," our caddie informed us. Of course! It would be a long flight across the desert to a food supply like Steve Wynn provides for them.

Let me describe for you three of Shadow Creek's par 3s. Number 5 was the first par 3 we encountered: 170 yards across a pine-tree-filled abyss. In fact, the hole is called "The Abyss." As they dug the Abyss, Steve Wynn kept saying "deeper, deeper" until they were 66 feet deep, with a tee box on one side and the green on the other. The Abyss is filled with mature pine trees. As I stood on the tee box, I could see the green on the opposite hillside surrounded by pine trees—not exactly a typical desert setting.

Number 8 looks like it belongs at Augusta National. Steve Wynn calls it "Shangri-La," inspired by the secret hideaway in the book *Lost Horizon*. Completely isolated from the rest of the course, the garden hole is 150 yards and filled with thousands of exotic flowers. You enter and leave it via entrance and exit tunnels. The experience was like walking into a painting. Shangri-La was one of the many surprises along the way.

Number 17 would be a signature hole on any golf course, but at Shadow Creek it is one of many signature holes. The 130-yard par-3 hole plays from a ridge 30 feet above the very small putting surface. It is framed in back by a massive waterfall cascading into a creek that drains into a lake in front of the green. Just close your eyes and imagine that for a moment. This particular creek was called Michael's Creek, named for Steve Wynn's father, and had a plaque to identify it. One of the first actions of the new owners was to remove the plaque and change the name of the creek. (It must have been a very friendly sale. Not!)

If my description of the course does not tell you that Steve Wynn thinks outside the box, then consider this: He submitted a bid for a major golf tournament. However, one of his stipulations was that the public would not be allowed on the course and 100 percent of the revenue would be generated by television. If that seems selfish and exclusionary of Wynn, then consider that Shadow Creek was the home course for the University of Nevada–Las Vegas golf team (it does not host the teams tournaments). Imagine being a college kid on the golf team with access to such an exclusive course.

After our round, we headed to the locker room. Sitting in front of our lockers were very shiny versions of our shoes. Jeff and Larry's shoes looked wonderful. I had worn gray bucks that day, and I kept looking at the third pair. They looked like mine, but they were shiny black. Finally I went to the shoe man: "These look like my shoes, but mine were gray bucks." He was very apologetic. "I looked and looked at your shoes trying to determine what color they were. I thought they might be bucks, so I tried suede cleaner. Nothing happened, so I concluded that they were black leather." He apologized again and said I could get compensated for the shoes, or the black polish could be stripped out. I wasn't mad, just stunned. We had a drink in the bar, and the more I looked at my shoes the better I liked them. In fact, I was coming to the conclusion that it was a dramatic improvement. So I went back to the locker room to thank the shoe man. He gave me a can of black shoe polish. I still have those shoes, and I still prefer them in black.

Shadow Creek is a wonderland. I know $500 is a lot of money, but not in Vegas economics, where people lose more than that in the casinos in minutes. It was well worth the cost.

I had 12 courses to go; I'd be turning the corner to single digits soon. There were days when I thought I would never get this far. Yet my goal seemed so close, and sometimes I thought, "Oh, my God, what am I going to do when this is over? It's been such a big part of my life." I'd have to deal with that when I got there.

disconnections

BETHPAGE BLACK

No matter how badly you are playing, it is always possible to play worse.

—Thomas Mulligan, for whom the mulligan was named

One of the questions I get asked regularly is, "What was the hardest course to get on?" In an odd way, it has to be Bethpage Black. Connections couldn't help. My eight years of networking did no good. Everyone is in the public system with everyone else who wants to play here. In fact, someone from out of state is at a distinct disadvantage because the automated phone reservation system, which is how advance tee times are made at New York municipal courses, makes it almost impossible for a nonresident to get a tee time. So I did as so many others do to play there.

Bethpage Black is a municipal golf course run by the state of New York on Long Island about 15 miles east of La Guardia Airport. There are five courses at Bethpage Park: Black, Red, Blue, Green, and Yellow. The Black Course was designed by A.W. Tillinghast in 1936; many call it "Tillie's Last Hurrah." In 1997, the Black Course was on the Top 100. It fell off two years later, and in 2000, the course underwent a major renovation at the hands of Rees Jones. When I played it, it was in fantastic condition and ready for the U.S. Open that was to be played there the following year. Oh, did I tell you the cost? $31. Yep, that's $31 to tee it up where Tiger would be teeing it up a year later.

The reservation system at Bethpage Black is phone-automated and run by the state of New York. Need I say more? I did get through a few times, but I could never get a tee time or even figure out if there were any to be had on the day I was hoping to play. Many automated phone menus later, I reached the pro shop and talked to the head pro. "I have nothing to do with the golf course or tee times," he said, "but I can tell you what you need to do if you want to play here. Show up at 5 a.m., or earlier, get in line, and hope for a cancellation or one of the very first times of the day that they save for walkups. And you better do this on a Tuesday, Wednesday, or Thursday, because that won't be nearly early enough on the weekend."

Every night, golfers arrive in the parking lot at Bethpage golf courses. They drive to numbered parking stalls and camp out for the night in their cars. They can't leave, or they'll lose their place in line. At 4 a.m., a park ranger comes around and gives these golfers a number. At 5 a.m., they drag their tired butts out of their cars and line up according to their numbers, followed by those who showed up in the morning, like poor old me, who got there at 5:15 a.m. I was in a line behind about 40 players, and the conversations I had with the people in line near me made it clear that these guys do this regularly. This is how they play golf. That's dedication! When I want to make a tee time at my home club, I pick up the phone, and three minutes later it's a done deal.

People were making tee times for all of the courses at Bethpage Park that day. There were a couple twosomes and maybe a threesome. If you're playing with friends, they'd better be in line with you; if they're not, they aren't getting a tee time. Don't even think about showing up late to join your friend in line. Cutting this line would be suicide. I was sweating it out, hoping beyond all hope that there was one single spot for me on the Black Course. I couldn't imagine what I would do if I were turned away and had to fly back here to try another day. Twelve courses to go was flashing in my mind, as were thoughts like, "I must be nuts."

When I finally got to the front of the line, at 6:00 a.m., I had a 10:30 time and four-and-a-half hours to kill. I made friends with the starter as best I could (he was a busy guy), and at 10, there was a cancellation. "Grab your clubs," he said, "you're up." I met my three playing partners: Joe, Cal, and John. I'd had plenty of time to get familiar with the scorecard. There were three yardages to choose from: Red, 6,265 yards; White, 6,773 yards; and Blue, 7,399 yards. I didn't see any women out here, and with 6,265 being the shortest tee boxes, I can see why. Ouch! But there are four other courses here that are more women-friendly. The Black Course is probably the sternest test of golf on a municipal course in the United States. In fact, there is a big sign by the starter that clearly states: WARNING: THE BLACK COURSE IS AN EXTREMELY DIFFICULT COURSE WHICH IS RECOMMENDED ONLY FOR HIGHLY SKILLED GOLFERS. But since the announcement that the U.S. Open would be played here, this may have been the most ignored sign in New York next to "Buckle Up for Safety."

I chose the white tees, as did Joe, Cal, and John, and we were off. It was damp and even a bit chilly and threatening rain. By the time we walked up the 18th fairway more than five hours later, the drizzle was beginning.

Of all the par 4s, only four were less than 400 yards and many were 420, 430, and 440, too long for me. But it is a beautifully designed course and in very good shape. Just how it stays in such good condition when it gets played from dawn to dusk every day is a mystery to me. It has lots of elevation changes, many heroic carries over fescue to the fairways and small heavily bunkered greens. In fact, the bunkers give this course its character. A WWII veteran once wrote, "I have seen no bomb craters that I've studied as anxiously as that bunker guarding Number 2 of the Black Course. They do come bigger. When the ruins are cleared away, plenty of them look more like the third hole from tee to green."

Long, thick rough abuts the fairways, with long fescue and many trees just outside of that. The Black Course demands long accurate play to small, well bunkered greens. My playing partners had played the Bethpage courses often and were very proud that the U.S. Open would be played on "their" home course. They were all blue-collar workers from Long Island who loved to golf in their free time. Two of them were night-shift workers who often stopped at Bethpage to play golf when they got off work.

No comment on how the front nine went, but I shot a 45 on the back and was damn proud of it. My short game was on through the back because most of the par 4s were unreachable for me. At 4 p.m., I was on my way to La Guardia for my flight home. I was glad I didn't have to go through this to play golf every day.

barnstorming, part 2

People talk about signature holes. That's not my thing. My belief is that every hole needs to be a signature hole; every golf course is a signature golf course.

—*Tom Fazio, course designer*

VICTORIA NATIONAL

Victoria National was the last course on a three-day trip with Jeff May. We flew into Evansville, Indiana, and I didn't really know what to expect. I was trying to figure out why someone had made such a great effort to build a top-notch golf course in Evansville, the southernmost city in Indiana, right on the Tennessee border.

Victoria National is one of the courses that I was able to get on with a phone call from the pro at my club. It was founded by Terry Friedman, who had bought a former coal mine with a golf course in mind. If you had asked me whether I was in favor of strip-mining a few weeks before my visit, I would have said, "No way." But I have seen what Tom Fazio did with a former strip mine, and it's fantastic. This is a tremendous example of turning lemons into lemonade.

Tom Rose, the head pro who would be playing with Jeff and me, filled us in on strip-mining. Long stripper pits are cut into the ground about 50- to 100-feet wide. The coal is pulled out in the process, and dirt (called spoils) is piled in huge mounds alongside the pits. In most cases, the digging continues until the water table is reached. What's left behind after the mining? Lots of elevation changes (from the spoils) and lots of water running through the property. Tom Fazio had turned this lump of coal into a diamond at Victoria National.

Victoria National has only 52 bunkers, but it has 114 different tee boxes. Relatively small amounts of dirt were moved here, and water comes into play on 15 holes, so sand bunkers become less relevant under those circumstances. Many of the holes run parallel to the spoils mounds, which creates lots of privacy from hole to hole.

The cart paths are almost invisible (due to Fazio's great skill), and people paths make this a very walkable course. The course is not connected with any housing development, which is unusual in golf-course construction today.

The stripped land has not been without problems. It was spongy, which was treated by top-dressing the fairways and greens with sand. On Number 15, for example, the sprinkler head was clearly two inches below the surface of the grass. Now the fairways and greens are in fantastic condition. Tom Fazio told me that all it took was one look at the land and the vision was clear to him. He also said it had been Terry Friedman's dream to get a USGA Championship from day one. He courted USGA officials mercilessly, until finally Victoria National held the USGA Senior Amateur in September 2006. Terry had since passed away, but I am sure he had a very proud family standing on the tee box at opening day of that competition.

I didn't play my best at Victoria National, but I remember standing on the 16th tee after I hit my tee shot into a stripper pit and declaring proudly that it was the first ball I had lost that day. Terry made me feel a little better when he said that the first time he played Victoria National he lost seven balls. Today Terry shot two under par. It was quite an improvement for him and quite a day for both Jeff and me. I loved this course, and it is easily in my Top 10.

the final countdown

SHORE ACRES

Big greens and big ravines.
—*Anonymous*

Shore Acres lies on the shore of Lake Michigan in the northern Chicago suburb of Lake Bluff, Illinois, roughly 15 miles south of the Wisconsin border. My friend Bob Milbourne played a lot of golf with Johnny Koss, Jr., before he moved to Columbus, and he introduced us. Johnny was on a quest closely related to mine. He had compiled a database of every golf course that had ever been listed on the *Golf Digest* Top 100, and he was on a quest to play them all. He's still working on it.

Johnny and his dad, John Koss, Sr., picked me up at the Milwaukee airport, and we drove the 50 miles to Shore Acres. We arrived around noon. Earlier that morning, Shore Acres had been host to the United States Senior Golf Association (USSGA). When we walked into the restaurant to meet Dan Ferguson, a longtime friend of John, Sr., and our host for the day, we found that the restaurant was filled with USSGA members who were just sitting down to lunch. I ran into Kim Whitney, my friend from Minneapolis. I proudly informed him that after today's round I would have only eight courses to go to reach my goal. The immensity of those words seemed surreal to me.

Shore Acres is Number 87 on the Top 100, but it deserves a higher ranking. The course was designed in 1921 by Seth Raynor, who has two other courses on the Top 100, Camargo and Fishers Island. (I had played one other Seth Raynor course, Somerset in St.

Paul.) Raynor worked with Charles Blair Macdonald on the design of National Golf Links of America, but quickly broke out on his own. He was one of the early masters at taking strategic design principles from famous holes in Scotland and adapting them to the terrain of his courses. In addition to distinctive design features, the four Seth Raynor courses I've played all had only 150 to 200 members. It's probably just a coincidence, but it could be a conspiracy to keep the general public from playing his excellent designs. A few weeks earlier, I had played Camargo, in Ohio, which is revered by students of classic golf-course architecture. At Camargo, my host told me about a golfer who shot a 59 during a round of match play. Fifty-nine would have been the course record, but match play cannot be counted as a course record because putts can be conceded. I asked if there was a course record for women, he pondered for a moment and shot back with 2 hours 15 minutes.

Big greens are a prominent feature of Raynor's courses; his greens often are square or rectangular in shape and sit on raised plateaus that appear flat, or almost flat, at first glance. Looks, however, are deceiving; the breaks are subtle and can leave your first putts a long way from the hole if you're not careful. The par-3 6th hole at Shore Acres is a perfect example: Here, the green is more than 200 feet deep (the equivalent of 70 yards, or three-fourths of a football field). There isn't a field-goal kicker in the NFL who could make a field goal of that length. Depending on pin placement, there could be a five- or six-club difference in club selection. Big greens are not specific to Shore Acres. At the Raynor-designed Camargo, the practice green was closed, so two practice holes were cut on the back of the 18th green, which didn't seem to interfere with play in the least.

There are significant elevation changes on Shore Acres, mostly in the form of ravines, with a few on the front nine and several on the back nine. Thank goodness for our great caddie! He knew what club we needed and where to aim every time. Knowing your carry distances is crucial here because the bottom of one of these ravines is not a good place to be. Some of these ravines have mowed, playable areas at the bottom, and one even has a patch mowed to fairway length, but for the most part, if you hit into one, it's kiss your ball goodbye. If you've read *Golf in the Kingdom*, you'll know what I mean when I say that some of those ravines on the back nine could be the home of Seamus McDuff.

At Shore Acres, the lake breezes definitely come into play. Oddly, the clubhouse is the only place at the club that is directly exposed to the lake, and you can't see the lake from anywhere on the golf course. The course is a short 6,377 yards from the tips, but they are a very challenging 6,377 yards.

FISHERS ISLAND

Columbus went around the world in 1492. That isn't a lot of strokes when you consider the course.

—Lee Trevino

Fishers Island New York is not only exclusive, but extremely remote as well. Unless you go by air, you can't get there from New York. The only other option is a ferry from New London, Connecticut—a ferry, I might add, that doesn't run on a convenient schedule. It's rare that a club as old as Fishers Island is just coming onto the *Golf Digest* Top 100. It had been on the list decades ago, and then it no longer wanted to be on the list, so it stopped inviting panelists. It took quite a while to persuade Fishers Island to re-rate its course, and several more years to convince the panelists to make the ferry trip to do it. I found it interesting that Fishers Island is in New York State, but actually much closer to Connecticut. When the island was first settled, the laws of New York were more favorable to the fishermen who lived there than Connecticut laws, so the islanders chose New York.

I was staying with Barclay Douglas, and he tagged along with me to Fishers Island. We left his house in a Boston suburb at 8:30 in the morning and drove one-and-one-half hours to New London, just barely making the ferry. We left the car at the ferry dock and hopped on the boat for a beautiful 45-minute ride in patchy fog.

Despite the calming effect of the ferry ride, I worried that we would be playing golf in the fog or, worse, that we would get weathered out of our round altogether. As we reached the shore, the fog began to clear, and by our 1:20 p.m. tee time we had good weather and good visibility. A policeman at the dock watched everyone disembark. I was told later by a colleague of mine who is playing the

Top 100 in the world that the policeman's purpose is to insure that there is a member or resident of the island there to meet each passenger who gets off the ferry. If no one is there to meet you, he personally puts you on the return boat to New London. How's that for exclusive?

Our hosts, Winn Hotchkiss, Sr., and Jr., met us at the Fishers Island ferry dock in their 1987 dusty green Buick. I was introduced to Winn, Sr., through my Minneapolis friend Kim Whitney, who came through with some terrific connections as I closed in on the last 20 percent of my goal. We stopped at the driving range to hit balls, then we picked up carts at the golf shop and headed down the path to eat lunch at what I thought was the pool house. But when we went around the building to sit down and order, there was the beach. Why not? If you have to decide between a pool and the ocean, the ocean seems like a pretty easy choice. The beach was crowded, as was the restaurant, but the food choices were quite limited. I scanned the menu and knew immediately what I was having for lunch that day. How often do you see a peanut butter, jelly, and bacon sandwich on a menu?

Fishers Island was designed by Seth Raynor in 1926. Similar to Shore Acres and Camargo, the course features those trademark Seth Raynor greens that almost look like they are sitting up on benches. Yet the large, raised, geometric-shaped greens are in perfect harmony with the ocean horizons, and you can see the ocean from nearly all of the fairways. Neither the fairways nor the rough at Fishers Island are watered. Only the tees and greens are irrigated, so the fairway conditions are completely dependent on rainfall and weather. When we played the course, the grass was dormant and your lie, even in the fairway, was a chancy thing. If you land in a divot, too bad; divots might not grow back until there's enough rain. As on Shore Acres, there are many ravines, so you'd better know the distances necessary to carry them. The rough is surrounded by gorse, making Fishers Island feel very much like a links course of Scotland—especially with views of the Long Island Sound on 15 of 18 holes. There's only one fairway bunker, which I noticed because I was in it. It was a calm day, which is unusual on this course, and with the dormant grass on the fairways, you could get lots of roll. When the wind blows, we were told, this course gets some serious teeth in it.

One thing I have come to expect at exclusive clubs is distinctive clubhouses and locker rooms. Fishers Island has no locker room. On the front wall of the golf shop are a couple dozen cubbyholes. That's it for locker room facilities: You simply leave your street shoes in a cubbyhole.

According to the pro, the club has approximately 450 members, which shoots my theory about Seth Raynor courses having small memberships. But the remoteness adds an element here: Most members, he said, come for only a week or two each year, so the course is rarely crowded. The last two weeks of August are the exception and the only time of the year a tee time is necessary.

I didn't like the lack of fairway conditioning. Other than that, most of the holes are spectacular because of their views of Long Island Sound, the Yacht Club, and Long Island. Barclay loved Fishers Island, and he should have. He shot 73, but he likes to tell how he couldn't sink his two-footer on 18 because it was 5:45 and we had to run off the course to make the last ferry of the day at 6 p.m.

200

a golfer's dream

you've got mail

The following emails contain my final thoughts as I moved ever closer to completing my quest for the Top 100.

SEPTEMBER 11, 2001

It is almost impossible to remember how tragic a place the world is when one is playing golf.

—Robert Lynd

September 11, 2001 was my 55th birthday, one I will never forget. A friend called me at home in the morning and said, "Turn on the TV." Like most people, I was glued to the media for the entire day. At the end of the late edition of the local news, Don Shelby, a longtime Twin Cities news anchor, shared his memories of the assassination of President John F. Kennedy. His basketball coach had refused to cancel basketball practice that night, and the next morning his father went back to work. He recalled how thankful he had been for those decisions. "Terrorism, like we experienced today, wins when we let the fear take over and alter our lives and infringe on our freedom," Shelby said. His message really hit home. It made me even more thankful for the freedoms I have, the friends I have, and the blessings I have in my life. I have tried to remember those things, as I face the horrors that have plagued our country in these past days. I can't help but think about how irrelevant it is when my anxiety rises over a bad golf shot. And I am reminded of how lucky I am to be able to enjoy the simple pleasures of golf and the life I experience every day.

As you know, my wife is a flight attendant for Northwest Airlines. Whenever there is a plane crash, she feels the same anxiety that many airline employees experience in returning to work immediately after such accidents. In August of this year, she was offered and accepted the option of a four-month leave from her job. I can't even begin to explain the relief we both feel that she did not have to go to work during these next few weeks.

As we all reflect on the past few days, let's ask ourselves if there's anything we've always wanted to do, anything that we've been putting off for another day. Then let's get out there and do it. There's no telling how long our dreams may be possible.

THANKSGIVING 2001

You're only here for a short visit. Don't hurry, don't worry. And be sure to smell the flowers along the way.

—Walter Hagen

I'd like to wish you all a Happy Thanksgiving. This is a special day in light of the events of September 11. We have counted and recounted our blessings and come closer together as a country and as family and friends. To you, my golf friends, with whom I have shared my quest to play the Top 100, I want to say how thankful I am for your support. The game of golf has changed my life. Golf has brought a rich array of friends from near and far into my life. Golf has taught me many life skills, such as patience, integrity, and concentration. It has given me great satisfaction to bring the game and its disciplines to underprivileged kids who would not otherwise experience the game. Golf has allowed me to walk in some of the most beautiful places in the world. Golf has given me many fulfilling solitary hours of practice outside on warm sunny days. Unfortunately, the weather today (at least here in Minnesota) is not warm or sunny, but it's a perfect day for reading about it. Here are my accounts of the 94th and 95th courses on my quest.

GRANDFATHER MOUNTAIN

Golf combines two favorite American pastimes: taking long walks and hitting things with a stick.

—P.J. O'Rourke

It's a beautiful day in the Allegheny Mountains of North Carolina. Ann and I are in Linville, home of Grandfather Golf and Country Club at the base of Grandfather Mountain. It took us a few hours to drive from Charlotte over the twisting mountain roads, but the drive was worth it. Grandfather Mountain, designed in 1968 by Ellis Maples, is the third Maples course I've played. He's a brilliant designer who's never gotten enough acclaim.

It's peak leaf weekend here in the Allegheny Mountains, the temperature is a sunny 65 degrees, and the colors surrounding this special golf course are brilliant. The course meanders up and down foothills at the base of Grandfather Mountain, with many streams winding through the trees. There are wonderful elevation changes on this course and the greens are very challenging—sometimes too challenging. You have to know where to put the ball to keep it below the hole. I three-putted six times and Ann had almost as many. It's hard to really pick out the most beautiful hole, but Number 7 really got our attention. After a slightly downhill tee shot that puts you at the bottom of the valley, you look up to see the fall splendor of Grandfather Mountain topped by a swinging bridge at its peak. What a view!

The club is private, but I got on simply by calling the head pro. If you are ever in North Carolina, make a call and see if you can get on. It's well worth it. We stayed nearby, and the next day we hiked a while on the Appalachian Trail. After lunch we went to the Woolly Worm Festival in Banner Elk to watch hundreds of woolly worms racing up four-foot-tall strings. At the end of the day, the winner has the honor of predicting the weather for the coming winter according to the width of its bands.

WADE HAMPTON

I know I am getting better at golf because I'm hitting fewer spectators.

—Gerald Ford

While the pro allowed us to play at Grandfather with just a phone call, Wade Hampton was not nearly as inviting. My host warned me not to show up before he did because the club doesn't allow unaccompanied guests on the grounds. Wade Hampton is in Cashiers, North Carolina, where the rich of Atlanta, eastern Tennessee, and Florida come to escape the summer heat. It's another fine fall day, and Wade Hampton is another fabulous course designed by Tom Fazio. Fazio has 10 courses on the Top 100, more than any other architect, and I loved Shadow Creek, Victoria National, World Woods, and Black Diamond Ranch—all of which he designed. Since Fazio lives in Hendersonville (about 40 minutes from here), I had to ask if Fazio might be at the club today. His wife was playing, as it turns out, but not Tom.

Several years ago when I played at Seminole with Kim Whitney, he brought along his friend from Chattanooga, Scott Probasco, who said to me, "Have you ever met a member from Wade Hampton? Well, you have now." I had to call him a few times—I think he really wanted me to play there when he could join me—but he finally hooked me up with a realtor friend of his who lived in Cashiers and was a member at Wade Hampton. When Annie, who had decided she didn't want to play today, dropped me off at the clubhouse, our host meekly said, "Please don't come back for at least four hours. They don't like unaccompanied strangers hanging around the clubhouse." In my opinion, this place protects its privacy too much.

Wade Hampton is set up in two very different mountain valleys. The holes had generous landing areas, but plenty of trouble around the greens. As my host drew his approach shot toward the pin on Number 1, he announced in his Southern drawl, "That ball had good towards, which is better than havin' yonders." The par 3s are wonderful: Number 6 is a short downhill over a stream surrounded by water, and Number 17 is very interesting with two steward trees that look like goalposts in front of what looks like an average-size flat green until you get up there and see that it's gigantic and far from flat. It's one of the most challenging greens on the course. After the turn I heard that Tom Fazio—a man I would love to meet—had come by to pick up his wife. I'd just missed him.

I have just five courses to go: the Quarry at La Quinta, Atlantic Golf Club, Baltimore Country Club, Winged Foot, and the Homestead. I am going to finish my quest next year! I plan to play the Quarry this winter, Atlantic, Baltimore and Winged Foot in early summer, and finish up at the Homestead in midsummer. Homestead in Virginia is a resort, and anyone who wants to join me on my 100th course is invited to do so. After No.100, I will host one or two celebrations and you all will be invited.

a golfer's dream

the back six

THE QUARRY AT LA QUINTA

The most rewarding things you do in life are often the ones that look like they cannot be done.

—*Arnold Palmer*

My friend Johnny Koss and his dad came through for me again and introduced me to a member at the Quarry at La Quinta. With their help, I was able to play the Quarry with Jim Fitzgerald, who is from Janesville, Wisconsin. His Palm Springs winter home is the Vintage Club, which was once on the Top 100. According to Mick Humphreys, developer of the Vintage Club and our fourth for golf at the Quarry, Vintage Club fell off the list when it was turned over to membership. His theory is that clubs run by benevolent dictators (i.e., developers) are kept up better than clubs that have been turned over to memberships.

I drove from Phoenix to Palm Springs with Jeff May to play the Quarry. Course architect Tom Fazio had created Black Diamond Ranch in Florida in a quarry and Victoria National in Evansville, Indiana, in a strip mine, so I expected this course to be made from an old quarry. I was wrong, but the Quarry is noteworthy in other ways. Along with Double Eagle in Columbus, Ohio, it may be one of the best conditioned courses I've ever played. Most greens in the West are bent grass; most greens in Florida are Bermuda grass. Golfers tend to prefer bent grass because it is far less grainy. The Quarry's greens are a new strain of Bermuda and they putt like bent grass. They're simply fantastic. Our group had a forecaddie who not only sanded every divot with green sand/seed mixture, but he picked up the divot pieces after each shot and put them in a bag that he disposed of at the end of the round. The fairways were spotless.

The Vintage Club, where we met Mick and Jim for breakfast, is exclusive, beautiful, and expansive. The Quarry is small, just 54 home lots, and very expensive to join: $225,000 initiation for an individual membership; your wife's membership privileges will cost another $225,000. The course has many elevation changes and generous, beautifully sculpted fairways in a breathtaking mountain setting. Number 8, a 138-yard par 3, must be as far down off the cliff as it is long. Four beautifully hit 9-irons yielded four pars. Fortunately, Number 9, a 614-yard par 5, was slightly downhill and downwind the day we played. Tom Fazio is my favorite golf architect, and the Quarry is a great course, but not nearly his best.

Jim Fitzgerald was in the cable TV business in Wisconsin and is a former owner of the Milwaukee Bucks and the Golden State Warriors. He also owns Softspikes, and according to Jim, the "Black Widow" Softspikes have 110 percent of the gripping power of metal spikes and are made of such durable material they don't wear out fast enough, which cuts into sales. "Greed is a wonderful thing," Fitzgerald said as he explained his marketing challenge. The company also had introduced a product called Laser Link, which uses laser guns aimed at pin reflectors to measure yardage. I've used similar devices, but Laser Link picked up the target unbelievably fast. Of course, these don't compare with the new Sky Caddie.

Our fourth, Mick Humphreys, played for the Oregon University golf team years ago and during his four years on the team OU was Pac-10 champion every year. Mick's probably a scratch golfer, although he shot a 79. It was a pleasure to watch him play the course the way it should be played. He was also the developer of Crosswater in Bend, Oregon.

Ninety-six courses down and four to go: Atlantic Country Club, Winged Foot East, Baltimore Country Club, and Cascades Golf Club at the Homestead in Hot Springs, Virginia.

DESERT FOREST

I traded one addiction for another, but golf is the crack cocaine of sports. Once I took it seriously I never tired of playing. It absolutely saved my life.

—Alice Cooper, musician and 5.3 handicap

Actually, I have four-and-two-thirds courses to go. Several years ago, I played Desert Forest in Carefree, Arizona. After six holes, it began to hail and play was halted. A week later, I was at the club again and the weather was so bad we never started—hard to imagine in Arizona! I later lost contact with that gracious host, but I was determined to complete the course. John Stringer, a friend from Minneapolis, said his father-in-law was a member at Desert Forest and he called him for me. So I played with Ed Morgan, a retired 3M VP of sales and then mayor of Carefree. Everyone at Desert Forest knew the mayor and greeted him.

Desert Forest, designed in 1952 by Red Lawrence, may have the most challenging greens in the Phoenix area. Although I love fast greens, these may be too hard. The course had been renovated recently by Tom Weiskopf, who pulled out all the non-native vegetation (more than 125 trees were removed). The bent grass fairways were also pulled up and Bermuda grass was put in (most courses in Arizona overseed with rye grass during the winter). Since the Bermuda grass was still "growing in," the course could not be overseeded for at least two years. So Desert Forest was a Top 100 course with brown fairways. The ball rolled and sat up, and it was an easy surface to play, but when I hit a good drive down the middle and heard, "Good shot. You're in the brown stuff," it sounded a little strange. Although I had a great time with Ed and our foursome, I don't believe this difficult and nondescript course rates Top 100 billing. Many of the courses that have fallen off the Top 100 in the past few years are much more appealing to me than Desert Forest. However, you should know these few things about Desert Forest. It has no out of bounds (today almost every golf course built in a housing development has out of bounds on most of its holes). It has no fairway bunkers, and it has no water hazards. This course was carved from the existing desert landscape with virtually no soil having been moved during construction. This is a far cry from the modern-day processes of golf-course design, where fairways and greens are contoured by moving tons of dirt. It is a bit like Sand Hills in that regard, which also moved almost no dirt in its construction process.

Only four courses to go now: Baltimore Country Club, Winged Foot East, Atlantic Country Club, and the Cascades Club at the Homestead.

—Sam Snead

CASCADES CLUB AT THE HOMESTEAD RESORT

If people gripped a knife and fork as poorly as they do a golf club, they'd starve to death.

Annie and I spent three days at the Homestead in Hot Springs, Virginia. The Homestead, established in 1766, is a mountain resort a few hundred miles from Washington, D.C. It is home to three golf courses, including Cascades Golf Club, which was designed by William Flynn in 1924 and ranks No. 48 on the Top 100. William Flynn is not exactly a household name in golf architecture, but he has two other courses on the Top 100: Cherry Hills in Denver and Shinnecock Hills on Long Island. It's a challenge to get to the Homestead if you don't live within driving distance of it. We flew to Roanoke and then drove an hour-and-a-half to get there. But it was well worth the time and effort, and I would recommend it to anyone, especially families. There's plenty to do other than golf. The rooms were wonderful, the food delicious and abundant, and if that weren't not enough, 18 United States Presidents—from George Washington to Bill Clinton—have stayed at the Homestead.

It's amazing that Cascades stays on the Top 100 at only 6,679 yards (par 70), but it's a challenging 6,679 yards with a rating of 73 and a slope of 137. The first few holes are very plain. On the third tee, Annie and I looked at each other and wondered how the course rated Top 100 status. We never asked ourselves that again, because the course just kept getting better and better. Tee-shot accuracy is essential. In addition to the overall elevation changes, there are many fairways with severe left and right elevation changes as well; a drive landing in the wrong spot could easily cause your ball to roll all the way across the fairway into the rough on the other side. You could spend a lot of time looking for a golf ball that you were sure was right under your feet. Cascades has five wonderful par 3s (including the closing hole, which is unusual) and only three par 5s, but the par 5s are fantastic—especially 16 and 17, which have a creek running through them and spectacular mountain ridges on either side. The greens were in great condition for so early in the season.

No trip to the Homestead would be complete without mention of Sam Snead, who had a hilltop home about a mile from the Cascades course. He was born nearby and was raised playing golf at the Homestead. He spent a lot of time at the Homestead as well as the Greenbriar resort, which is less than an hour away. Unfortunately, I never saw Sam Snead when we were there, but I ate at Sam Snead's restaurant and learned a lot about him from the memorabilia on the wall, including the following facts: He recorded 33 holes-in-one in his career. He won more PGA tour events (81) than anyone living or dead. He was the oldest person to win a PGA tour event, at the age of 53 (the senior tour did not exist until much later). He never won the U.S. Open, although he came in second four times. He won three Masters, three PGA Championships, and a British Open. (He also played on eight Ryder Cup teams.) He played much of his career before earnings statistics were recorded, but I think it's safe to say that Sam Snead's career winnings don't even come close to Tiger Wood's winnings for the last three months. They say he had the "sweetest swing in golf," which he demonstrated as the honorary starter at the 2002 Masters. He died a month later, just before his 90th birthday.

WINGED FOOT WEST

Winged Foot has a great mixture of members; you play one round with a schoolteacher and the next with a Wall Street CEO.

—*Rick Pitino, basketball coach*

Several years after I played Winged Foot East, I finally got an invitation to play the West course. I played with a friend I'd met through the Shivas Irons Society, Rob Williams, who brought along his friend Steven Rockefeller. Winged Foot was built 60 years ago. It has "a rambling stone clubhouse that might make one of its occasional visitors, the Duke of Windsor, feel homesick," Dan Jenkins said. All of the stone used in the clubhouse was quarried at the site. It's just as impressive inside with a two-level locker room of full-length, metal double-door lockers, each one of which is large enough to fit a full-sized man or perhaps a full-week's wardrobe. Dave Marr described it this way: "It is to golf what Yankee Stadium is to baseball or Wimbledon is to tennis." The total cost to build Winged Foot (300 acres of land for 36 holes, golf-course construction, and clubhouse construction) was $750,000.

The average green at Winged Foot is 5,100 square feet, small by today's standards. In his book about Winged Foot, Doug Smith says that there are basically two types of golf-course architecture: strategic and penal. Penal is basically one line to follow to your target; if you don't follow it, you're penalized. A strategic course is one where the golfer has several options to meet his goal, as long as the ball stays in play. Smith says both Winged Foot courses are classic strategic courses. The East course has more water and more doglegs than the West course. Many members swear the greens are tougher on the East, but the West hosts all the big championships and therefore gets all the notoriety. It's a busy place, but the club has a no-tee-time policy. Just show up and play. I had a good round, shooting in the low 90s and putting very well. By the fourth hole, all of us had chipped one in from off the green. By the end of the day, Steven had invited me to play golf at the private estate of his Rockefeller family, which I haven't had a chance to take him up on, but you can bet I will. Ninety-eight down, two to go.

BALTIMORE COUNTRY CLUB

As I look back at the friends made, beautiful places seen, and, yes, even improvements in my swing, I am pleased to have found this community of extraordinary diverse individuals pursuing our magnificent obsession.

—Reg Murphy, former president of USGA and Baltimore Country Club member

Every once in a while I meet someone that I really connect with on my quest. Bill Knott and I really hit it off the day I played No. 99, Baltimore Country Club. A friend of my cousin, A.J. Alper, had called his wife's uncle, Bill Knott. Bill was nice enough to be my host—so nice, in fact, that he picked me up at the train station. Bill is in his 60s and still a 6-handicap. I was a bit nervous about what he would expect, but I had no need to be. Bill kept trying to put together a foursome, but in the end it was just the two of us. I am so glad it turned out that way, because we got to know each other much better spending the day as a twosome.

Baltimore Country Club was designed by A.W. Tillinghast, who has several courses on the Top 100. He is also credited with Bethpage Black, but recent evidence seems to refute that. He most certainly designed Baltimore and did an outstanding job. Baltimore Country Club is 102 years old, although this particular course was not built for the club until 1926 and has hosted five major championships. All of the holes have been named, and those names clearly (if not poetically) describe each hole. Number 4, a par 3 called Plateau, has a huge green sitting high on a plateau. A few holes later is a par-5 dogleg left called the Barn. In its June 2006 issue, Sports Illustrated rated 18 of Tillinghast's best holes. Number 6 and Number 14 (called Hell's Half Acre), both par 5s, made that list. The course is beautiful—definitely one of Tillinghast's best—mostly because of the way it relates to the trees (something that Tillinghast probably had very little to do with). Greens are set in forested amphitheaters that frame the holes, but you never feel like you're on tree-lined fairway after tree-lined fairway. Number 17, the final par 3, is called Picturesque. Enough said.

For me, Baltimore was about learning and laughing. Bill would mention something he'd read in a golf book, and then we'd try it out on the course. We had a terrific day together, and I was back to being the best guest I could possibly be. He shot 72 (4 under his handicap), and I shot 93 (a couple OBs did me in), but I really noticed a big improvement in my game. Bill came to visit me in Minneapolis a couple of years later and now has a winter home in Phoenix not far from me. We have become very good friends and play lots of golf together. He and his wife are even trying to teach me to play bridge.

—Byron Nelson

ATLANTIC GOLF CLUB

I still feel like one of these days I am going to be like Rip Van Winkle and wake up to find it's been a good long dream.

I did it! What an accomplishment! There have been days when I thought this 10-year journey would never end. My quest ended at Atlantic Golf Club on Sunday, July 16, 2002. Atlantic Golf Club is on Long Island in Bridgehampton. Designed in 1992 by Rees Jones, it is ranked No. 100, and that is a good spot for it. There's no doubt that Atlantic is great, but it's one of the least of all greats. I was lucky to have completed the Top 100 at this location. First, a Long Island newspaper published a story on my quest. Second, Long Island is the home of golf in the United States. Third, I played with two friends, Steve Rabolusky (who lives on Long Island) and Morgan Clawson (who is from Minneapolis). We were required to play with someone from the pro shop. Pro-shop assistant Rusty Ripenberger stepped up. The course record was 67 before we teed off, and Rusty shot 33/33 for 66, a course record (although he tried to play down its "officialness" because some of the tees were not all the way back). I took some photos on the 18th green and told Rusty I would email them to him. "What is your email address?" I asked. "Ripdog54@---," was his answer. Laughing, Morgan asked him if there had been 53 other Ripdogs before him when he registered that address. "No, that is my target golf score!" This kid's goal is to get out of the pro shop and onto the PGA tour. I hope he does.

On Monday, Morgan, my friend Dave Zubke, and I played National Golf Links, had lunch, and then played Shinnecock Hills—two fantastic courses. While Atlantic was wonderful, Shinnecock and National are real treasures. Morgan had bought a round at Shinnecock at a charity auction in Minneapolis. So our arrangement was that he would play Atlantic with me and I would play Shinnecock with Dave Zubke and him. Our host had said, "As long as you are here, let's play Shinnecock in the morning and National in the afternoon." What a way to celebrate the completion of this 10-year journey, completing it on a course that charges one-quarter of a million dollars to join and then playing two of the best courses in the world the next day. I am playing better. I had a good round at National, including a 43 on the back, and played pretty well at Shinnecock, even though it was a long and windy day. I can hardly believe I did it. It's a fantastic end to a journey, and a door, I am sure, will soon open to another one.

personal scorecard

Things I Learned Along the Way

· Golf is a metaphor for life. The things we live out on the golf course are a microcosm of the things we live out in life.

· Network, network, network. My considerable networking skills were sharpened on this quest. I started with a mailing list, sharing stories with those who were interested in my quest and those who had helped me or hosted me. The mailing list turned into an email list as email came into existence and the emails I sent became the basis of this book.

· People are thrilled to help. At first I was reluctant to ask people to help me. As time went on I found that most people, although certainly not all, were not only willing to help but excited to help me on this quest and others. I learned that it is human nature to want to help other people.

· Don't be afraid to introduce yourself to the big guys. You never know what fantastic second chances may crop up as a result.

· A great guest is always welcome. I tried to be as entertaining as I could be and put my hosts' enjoyment of the round ahead of concern for my score and certainly ahead of any frustration I experienced over bad shots. Their enjoyment of our round and our time together became more important to me than my score.

· Bad shots should be looked at as "opportunity shots." They create an opportunity to make a spectacular recovery. If you aren't in trouble in the first place, you don't have that opportunity.

· A course seen with a photographer's eyes is even more beautiful. When I played Maidstone with Evan Schiller, a golf-course photographer, we talked about what he looks for to create good golf-course photos and I began to see golf courses from a new perspective.

· I started teaching myself how to read yardage! When I played National Golf Links of America and found out there are no yardage markers on the course, I started learning how to read yardages. I would approach my ball, make my best guess, and then find a yardage marker to confirm (or not) what I estimated. My final drill was to play a round during which I would never look at the yardage, but simply trust my judgment, pull a club, and go for it. It didn't always go perfectly, but I had enough success that I impressed even myself.

· Repetition improves memory. I began to work on remembering the details of the holes I played at San Francisco Golf Club by reviewing all the previous holes I had played after finishing each hole. For example, on the 6th tee I went over my shots and details of holes 1 through 5. It worked! I remembered the golf course much better than I did courses I had played earlier.

· Never forget a name. I wrote everyone's names on my scorecard and referred to it when I forgot. People love it when you remember their names and address them regularly by name.

my top 10 favorite top 100 golf courses

(in no particular order)

Pebble Beach

Cypress Point

Merion

Oakland Hills

Muirfield Village

Victoria National

Black Diamond Ranch

Forest Highlands

The Sanctuary

Shinnecock Hills

Pebble Beach

Spyglass

National Golf Links of America

Winged Foot East

Prince Course Princeville Kauai

Kauai Lagoons

Desert Highlands

Pinehurst No. 2

Country Club of North Carolina

Black Wolf Run

Whistling Straits

Milwaukee Country Club

Valley Club of Montecito

Desert Mountain Renegade

Cog Hill

Shoal Creek

Grandfather Golf and Country Club

Interlachen

Hazeltine

Mauna Kea

Pasatiempo

The Estancia Club

Wade Hampton

Cascades at the Homestead

a golfer's dream

players club

MY FRIENDS AND GOLF PARTNERS WEIGH IN ON THE QUEST

New York State of Mind
by David Zubke

I am not sure I can ever play golf in New York again, as it will be tough to beat my first golf trip there with Larry and our mutual friend Morgan Clawson. Morgan had the foresight to support a local junior-golf charity with the top bid for lunch and a round of golf at Shinnecock Hills, one of the five founding clubs of the United States Golf Association. Our host, who is an avid golfer and retired executive, double-sweetened the chance of a lifetime when he suggested that we might also enjoy a round at one of the other area clubs he belonged to: the National Golf Links, which adjoins Shinnecock, both geographically and in most rankings as one of the top golf courses in the country.

Larry and Morgan were already summering in the Hamptons when I arrived early Sunday afternoon. I raced to Bethpage Black State Park, hoping to get out as a mid-afternoon single on the (in)famous Black course designed by A.W. Tillinghast and host a few weeks earlier of the 2002 U.S. Open. I had read and heard many stories over the years about the ordeal golfers go through to tee it up on the Black course, but hoped that the many available diversions in the city on such a spectacular summer day would leave a single spot open for me. Wrong. I sat in a line for between five and 10 minutes with other hopefuls and was crushed to learn that the Black course was not only booked solid, but had closed its single's waitlist until after 5 p.m., which was the approximate time I was supposed to be meeting my friends for dinner 70 miles away.

A few deep sighs and an hour-and-a-half later, I was in the parking lot of the Atlantic Country Club, a 1992 Rees Jones links design that was about to become Larry's final Top 100 course. This beautiful, traditional course and the quaint East Coast clubhouse were both designed to look like they had been part of the Hamptons since the late 1800s and not the last part of the 20th century, when a local developer spent somewhere around $23 million to turn rolling, inland farmland into a secluded playground for a few very well heeled city folk and, from time to time, select guests from around the country. We spent an hour or so at the Atlantic bar, watching the sunset and toasting Larry's accomplishments.

After an edgy night's sleep, we met our host for our morning round and lunch at Shinnecock. As we approached the pro shop, we noticed a sea of carts and brightly colored bags, but few men to be seen. We discovered quickly that Shinnecock was hosting a ladies' guest day that morning, with only the back nine open for other play. Plan B was quickly and decisively launched, and a few minutes later, we were changing shoes in the National's stone-fortress clubhouse just down the road. We spent the morning playing an incredibly scenic course and receiving an ongoing golf history lesson from our host, who provided many facts and amusing anecdotes as we walked the C.B. Macdonald replica/tribute holes imported from decades earlier.

Our next stop was the corner table of the Shinnecock clubhouse porch for an outdoor lunch facing what has to be one of the best golf views in America. Below and surrounding the classic shake-shingled clubhouse was a spectacular links course, grasses shining and swaying in the near constant summer breezes. Most of my afternoon walk is still a mental blur to me (probably blacked out by my golf psyche); the steady winds, thick, unyielding grasses, and slick, multi-contoured greens took their toll as I stumbled over one historic hole after another. Bogeys, doubles, and I think even an "X" or two. Approaches, not precisely hit, rolled this way or that, often into strategic bunkers or more devilish grassy areas. Drives not placed with precision in strategic landing areas provided more trouble and drama for a struggling amateur's game. And yet, with so much history and beauty, Shinnecock is unquestionably still one of the best golf walks I have ever been fortunate enough to take.

My glowing New York memories are topped by my outrageously lucky Hollywood golf-movie ending, produced and directed in large part by those evil island winds I had struggled with all afternoon. A 165-yard approach shot hit well right of the green got caught in a gust, moving and moving and moving ever closer to the green, finally settling pin-high and a few feet away for a tap-in birdie, burned into my mind in glorious slow motion, Southampton Technicolor.

Can I ever top this ending to a perfect golf day? Probably not, but Larry, you already know that I will dust off the Bermudas at a moment's notice, wherever and whenever you are ready to produce your next quest. Thanks again for unlocking all of those Top 100 clubhouse doors and for allowing me to serve as one of your Top 100 wingmen for some really great walks and even greater memories.

Anything Goes
by Marty Boxer

Almost any golf course is fine by me. I'm no snob. I've enjoyed $20 nine-hole munis as much as some $200 "name" tracks. A well struck shot on an Australian outback course with untended fairways and oiled-sand "greens" is still a pleasure and will bring a smile. That said, I certainly can appreciate the history, the beauty, and the challenge of a classic golf course. Some nights I can't sleep before a round on a special course.

Larry Berle's quest to play the *Golf Digest* Top 100 U.S. courses brought us together almost 10 years ago. I was living in Scottsdale, Arizona, at Desert Highlands, a Jack Nicklaus course that had hosted the first televised Skins Game with Watson, Player, Palmer, and Nicklaus. Desert Highlands had been in the Top 100 for about 10 years (it has since dropped out). Larry was doing a production with the Phoenix Symphony, where he met my cousin Joan and found a connection to play a course on the list.

I was happy to host Larry and his quest intrigued me. I had, of course, seen the *Golf Digest* list of the Top 100 and had ticked off the few I had played: Quaker Ridge, Pebble, Spyglass, and a half-dozen others. The challenge of playing the entire list seemed daunting. How to get on at Augusta National and at Cypress Point?

Larry was good company on the golf course that day at Desert Highlands, a good storyteller and a quick player. After the round we exchanged numbers and stayed in touch with email (updates on Larry's progress toward No. 100), holiday cards, and the occasional round of golf.

Memories of the Way It Was

by Larry Hoof

We played Troon North in Scottsdale, Arizona, in the early '90s before the Top 100 became The Quest. Troon must be one of the early desert-resort courses, punctuated by fairways interrupted by scrub and cactus. I remember hitting my approach shot to the 18th green at twilight, not knowing where it went, only to find it at the back edge of the green and finishing with a par! But golf with Larry and Ann is not all course work. We hopped the train up the Verde Valley to an old mining town one day and spent another delightful day at Taliesin West, the Frank Lloyd Wright retreat and school well outside of Phoenix (at that time, at least). Then, there was the green-pepper beer in the bar in Carefree.

On Super Bowl Weekend 1998, Larry and Ann had rented a house in Pacific Grove. Kathy and I accepted an open invitation to visit for a long weekend. It was most memorable. Our first round was played at a new course, designed by Fred Couples, and it was a beautiful day in January for a couple of Minnesota boys. We drove through Monterey, stopping at Pebble Beach, into the clubhouse, down to the 18th green to pay homage as the preparations were being made for the annual Pro-Am, down the 17-mile drive that dissects it, to a nearby beach at sunset. While walking the beach, I recovered more than a dozen "misplaced" golf balls that had left the fairways on the north side of the point. On Saturday, we were hosted at the Big Sur retreat: Esalen, Michael Murphy's creation and center for adult education. The lunch was organic, the hot water springs filled the cliffside soaking pools enjoyed au natural. On top of that was the full-body massage at sunset above the pounding surf.

The transformative power of golf is an important theme in Murphy's book *Golf in the Kingdom*. Larry had embraced the concepts, joined the Shivas Irons Society, and conducted fundraising events and golf outings. We spent an afternoon with the passionate director of the Society, Steve Cohen.

The golf at the Inn at Spanish Bay was so very different from anything I had experienced before. I clearly remember a par on the 1st hole (I play to over a 20 handicap) and the glow from a low sun reflecting off the endless surf. At the end of the round, at twilight, a lone bagpiper played while the players gathered in the bar for the end of the football game. Magical!

A week later, nearly everything changed. The storm interrupted the Pebble Beach Pro-Am, destroyed the cliffside pools at Esalen, and lay waste much of Big Sur. But we have our memories of how it was...

As a member of the Vashon Island Golf and Country Club, I was able to secure a tee time at Sahalee as it was set to host the PGA Championship in 1998. Larry made the trip to Seattle, and we caught a perfect Sunday afternoon in mid-April for exploring the tree-lined fairways of this challenging course. My regret was having an evening commitment that kept me from playing all of the 27 holes.

Larry was always inviting friends to join him as he set up rounds at the courses on the list. I was able to carve out a long-weekend holiday in Las Vegas with Kathy, using the round at Shadow Creek as the inspiration. Now, you gotta know that putting out $500 for a round of golf is an uncomfortable extravagance for me. But I found a way to justify it and earn the support of my wife as we had plenty of time to catch shows and entertainment. With Larry, we even got to the Liberace Museum!

The desert in January can be an unforgiving place. Our day, starting with the limousine ride, turned out to be high overcast and calm, temperatures in the mid-40s. I got to par the first hole! A phenomenally beautiful course and you would never know from a fairway that the property is in such a harsh desert environment.

I remember the Sunday at Sahalee as being mild, calm, and dry with occasional sun, unusual for an April day in the home of Microsoft (Redmond, Washington). Yes, the course was wet (damn ponds everywhere, it seems), and the ball didn't run far down the fairway (when I could find it). Later, in 1998, I volunteered for the PGA Championship, spent my volunteer hours in the media tent, captured autographs from Tom Lehman and Jim Furyk, and was safely at home when the deluge hit the course at the end of play on Sunday and V.J. Singh claimed the trophy.

I remember the night when Larry arrived home in Minneapolis with his bag of souvenirs and fresh stories of playing the par-3 course at Augusta. Oh, he got on the big course, too! I can see him floating about the room as he recalled the lush playground from the days before. I still have the pencil he gave me! I think it was then that he came to believe that he could actually continue and complete the quest!

I have known Larry since 1970. While there has been much time and distance between us over 36 years, we have always found a way to have delightful times in company, be it on the course, having dinner, out for a show, or exploring Hoover Dam. His energy and humor are always at a peak, it seems. And the people who know him are better for it.

how golf digest finds America's top 100 courses

The *Golf Digest* Course Rating Panel of more than 800 low-handicap men and women evaluates courses on seven criteria, each on a scale of 1 (Unacceptable) to 10 (Perfect). The categories, which apply to America's 100 Greatest Courses, America's 100 Greatest Public Courses, and Best in State are as follows:

1. Shot Values

   How well does the course pose risks and rewards and equally test length, accuracy, and finesse?

2. Resistance to Scoring

   How difficult, while still being fair, is the course for a scratch player from the back tees?

3. Design Variety

   How varied are the golf course's holes in differing lengths, configurations, hazard placements, green shapes, and green contours?

4. Memorability

   How well do the design features (tees, fairways, greens, hazards, vegetation, and terrain) provide individuality to each hole, yet a collective continuity to the entire 18?

5. Aesthetics

   How well do the scenic values of the course (including landscaping, vegetation, water features, and backdrops) add to the pleasure of a round?

6. Conditioning

   How would you rate the playing quality of tees, fairways, and greens when you last played the course?

7. Ambience

   How well does the overall feel and atmosphere of the course reflect or uphold the traditional values of the game?

From Golf Digest, May 2007
Golf Digest's America's Top 100 Golf Courses 2001/2002

America's 100 Greatest Golf Courses 2001-2002

		state	architect
1	Pebble Beach Golf Links	CA	Jack Neville & Douglas Grant
2	Pine Valley Golf Club	NJ	George Crump & H.S. Colt
3	Augusta National	GA	Alister Mackenzie & Bobby Jones
4	Cypress Point Club	CA	Alister Mackenzie & Robert Hunter
5	Oakmont CC	PA	Henry Fownes
6	Shinnecock Hills GC	NY	William Flynn
7	Merion GC (East)	PA	Hugh Wilson
8	Winged Foot Golf Club (West)	NY	A.W. Tillinghast
9	Pinehurst Resort (no.2)	NC	Donald Ross
10	Oakland Hills C.C. (South)	MI	Donald Ross
11	The Olympic Club (Lake)	CA	Sam Whiting
12	Seminole Golf Club	FL	Donald Ross
13	The Country Club (Clyde/Squirrel)	MA	Willie Campbell & Alex Campbell
14	Medinah CC (no.3)	IL	Tom Bendelow & Harry Collis
15	Southern Hills CC	OK	Perry Maxwell
16	National Golf Links	NY	C.B. Macdonald
17	Muirfield Village GC	OH	Jack Nicklaus & Desmond Muirfield
18	San Francisco GC	CA	A.W. Tillinghast
19	Crystal Downs CC	MI	Alister Mackenzie
20	Quaker Ridge GC	NY	A.W. Tillinghast
21	Riveria CC	CA	George C. Thomas
22	Los Angeles CC (North)	CA	George C. Thomas
23	Oak Hill CC (East)	NY	Donald Ross
24	Inverness Club	OH	Donald Ross
25	Cherry Hills CC	CO	William S. Flynn
26	Prairie Dunes CC	KS	Perry Maxwell

#	Course	State	Architect
27	Garden City GC	NY	Devereux Emmet
28	Baltusrol GC (Lower)	NJ	A.W. Tillinghast
29	Scioto CC	OH	Donald Ross
30	Olympia Fields CC (North)	IL	Willie Park Jr.
31	Shadow Creek	NV	Tom Fazio
32	Winged Foot Golf Club (East)	NY	A.W. Tillinghast
33	Peachtree GC	GA	Robert Trent Jones & Bobby Jones
34	Spyglass Hill	CA	Robert Trent Jones
35	Wannamoisett CC	RI	Donald Ross
36	Sand Hills GC	NB	Bill Coore & Ben Crenshaw
37	Wade Hampton GC	NC	Tom Fazio
38	Interlachen CC	MN	Willie Watson
39	The Golf Club	OH	Pete Dye
40	Colonial CC	TX	John Bredemus
41	Bandon Dunes	OR	David McLay Kidd
42	Maidstone Club	NY	Willie Park Jr. & Jack Park
43	Chicago GC	IL	C.B. Macdonald
44	Fishers Island Club	NY	Seth Raynor
45	Somerset Hills CC	NJ	A.W. Tillinghast
46	Bethpage Black	NY	A.W. Tillinghast
47	Plainfield CC	NJ	Donald Ross
48	Cascades G Cse	VA	William Flynn
49	Kitansett Club	MA	William Flynn & Frederic Hood
50	Milwaukee CC	WI	H.S. Colt & C.H. Alison
51	Prince Course	HI	Robert Trent Jones Jr.
52	Victoria National GC	IN	Tom Fazio
53	The Honors Course	TN	Pete Dye
54	Hazeltine National GC	MN	Robert Trent Jones
55	Sand Ridge GC	OH	Tom Fazio
56	Canterbury GC	OH	Herbert Strong

57	Baltimore CC (East)	MD	A.W. Tillinghast
58	Butler National GC	IL	George & Tom Fazio
59	Valley Club of Montecito	CA	Alister Mackenzie
60	East Lake GC	GA	Donald Ross
61	Laurel Valley GC	PA	Dick Wilson
62	Whistling Straits (Straits)	WI	Pete Dye
63	TPC Sawgrass (Stadium)	FL	Pete Dye
64	Cog Hill (No.4)	IL	Dick Wilson
65	Salem CC	MA	Donald Ross
66	Harbour Town Golf Links	SC	Pete Dye & Jack Nicklaus
67	The Ocean Course	SC	Pete Dye
68	Shoal Creek	AL	Jack Nicklaus
69	Desert Forest Golf Club	AZ	Red Lawrence
70	Black Wolf Run (River)	WI	Pete Dye
71	Congressional CC (Blue)	MD	Robert Trent Jones & Rees Jones
72	Crooked Stick GC	IN	Pete Dye
73	Bellerive CC	MO	Robert Trent Jones
74	Castle Pines GC	CO	Jack Nicklaus
75	Camargo Club	OH	Seth Raynor
76	Mauna Kea	HI	Robert Trent Jones
77	Pasatiempo GC	CA	Alister Mackenzie
78	Valhalla GC	KY	Jack Nicklaus
79	Grandfather G&CC	NC	Ellis Maples
80	Point O' Woods G&CC	MI	Robert Trent Jones
81	The Estancia Club	AZ	Tom Fazio
82	Sahalee CC (South/North)	WA	Ted Robinson
83	Black Diamond Ranch (Quarry)	FL	Tom Fazio
84	Jupiter Hills Club (Hills)	FL	George Fazio
85	NCR CC (South)	OH	Dick Wilson
86	Forest Highlands (Canyon)	AZ	Jay Morrish & Tom Weiskopf

87	Shore Acres	IL	Seth Raynor
88	Eugene CC	OR	Robert Trent Jones
89	Sanctuary GC	CO	Jim Engh
90	Double Eagle Club	OH	Jay Morrish & Tom Weiskopf
91	The Quarry at La Quinta	CA	Tom Fazio
92	Stanwich Club	CN	William and David Gordon
93	Long Cove Club	SC	Pete Dye
94	Sycamore Hills GC	IN	Jack Nicklaus
95	Greenville CC (Chanticleer)	SC	Robert Trent Jones
96	Crosswater	OR	Bob Cupp
97	World Woods (Pine Barrens)	FL	Tom Fazio
98	Aronimink GC	PA	Donald Ross
99	Wilmington CC (South)	DE	Robert Trent Jones
100	Atlantic GC	NY	Rees Jones

232

a golfer's dream